Essential Tools, Tips & Techniques *for the* Home Cook

Essential Tools, Tips & Techniques *for the* Home Cook

A Professional Chef Reveals the Secrets to Better Cooking

Michelle Doll

Culinary school teacher and owner of
Michelle Doll Makes

PAGE STREET
PUBLISHING CO.

First published in 2018 by
Page Street Publishing Co.
27 Congress Street, Suite 105
Salem, MA 01970
www.pagestreetpublishing.com

Distributed by Macmillan, sales in Canada by The Canadian Manda Group.

22 21 20 19 18   1 2 3 4 5

ISBN-13: 978-1-62414-550-6
ISBN-10: 1-62414-550-7

Library of Congress Control Number: 2018935800

Cover and book design by Kylie Alexander for Page Street Publishing Co.
Photography copyright © 2018 by Alexandra Grablewski

Printed and bound in China

Contents

Foreword

As the National Chef for Sur La Table, I have taught thousands of home cooks how to get comfortable in their kitchens. I have said one thing to each one of these students that has changed their cooking games forever: you cannot make anything taste good unless you start with incredible ingredients. The exact same thing is true when it comes to your kitchen tools. Without a flex boning knife, you will never be able to break down a chicken; without a firm spatula, your fish will fall apart in the pan; the wrong whisk will give you a blister and a good nonstick pan will make your cooking taste superhuman!

It is so true that anyone can be an amazing cook, but like anything you need a foundation. Sure, you might be able to wow a crowd with your famous lasagna or that one salad dressing recipe your mom gave you in college. Yet, without a base you will forever be stuck to those recipes and it will be impossible to reach your full culinary potential. We all know reaching your potential in anything takes the right support system. Without someone behind you acting as your coach, mentor and cheerleader, it's easy to fall short time and time again.

Michelle Doll is your kitchen guru! When it comes to building a solid foundation, your cooking goals can flourish. Michelle's relatable humor and ability to make even some of the most challenging kitchen tasks seem doable is why she has inspired so many to get behind the stove. Michelle has converted me to a lover of Silpats, changed the way I look at pie crusts and forever demystified pressure cookers to a point where I don't feel like I will blow up every time I use one. Like me, countless students at Sur La Table have benefited from Michelle's expertise and guidance and still look to her as the trusted authority when curating for our home and professional kitchens.

Yet finding the right cutting board or stand mixer is only the beginning! In this book, Michelle shares some of the most gorgeous tasting recipes, from Classic Fried Chicken (page 137) to her tender and delicious Grape Shallot Focaccia (page 90). Like her approach to curation, Michelle's goofiness and professional experience make the perfect mix to take on tons of recipes that you will use forever!

True, your cooking will fall flat without the right tools, recipes and mentorship. Just by picking up this book and following Michelle's lead, you are taking one giant leap toward achieving your cooking aspirations!

—**Joel Gamoran**

National Chef, Director of Culinary

Sur La Table

Introduction

I've been cooking and baking since I was a kid. The mechanics of it all fascinated me. How could you leave uncooked rice in a bowl of water indefinitely and nothing would happen but when you heat it up, BOOM—edible rice? I've also always been fascinated with the tools. Seeing someone wield a raclette cheese knife or a blowtorch had me hooked—the kitchen is where the action most definitely is.

I've been accumulating kitchen tools and cooking techniques my entire life, and after the thousandth request from a student or friend to help organize their kitchen or give them a list of the tools they absolutely must have and maybe a recipe or two to impress a date or an in-law, I decided that perhaps a book was in order. You don't need every newfangled, shiny kitchen tool, but having a few high-quality basics will give you everything you need to put some amazing food on your table. Of course, you need the techniques too. It's not just about recipes; as you read through the recipes in this book, I want you to think about what each ingredient is contributing and how you would personalize that recipe to make it your own. Want to add pumpkin pie spice to the Dutch baby recipe? There's nothing stopping you! Want to try it with almond milk? Go for it. I'm not guaranteeing that substituting everything will work 100 percent of the time, but more often than not they will, and that's what makes cooking fun—making things your own. It turns every meal into a gift for yourself or the people you love, or the people you can't stand but had to invite over because they just moved in down the block and hey, why not impress them? If we all like good food, maybe they aren't so bad and ohmygosh good food could = world peace. Why didn't we think of this before? Clean out your kitchens of the useless gizmos and thingamajigs that are taking up valuable space and start cooking for each other.

Michelle Doll

Chapter 1

This Is How I Roll

On Pins and Noodles

From the way you clean your rolling pin to the type of butter you choose, a number of factors affect the quality of your dough. First, let's talk about the pin. There are approximately 5,289 different kinds of rolling pins available, but only one that you absolutely must have. Let's review some of the possibilities.

The Best Tools for the Job

Tapered French Rolling Pin

RECOMMENDED OR NOT: Yes! Every cook should have one.

PROS: Good if you have trouble making round circles of dough or have arthritis, as you can apply more pressure to one side to get the desired effect. Easy to store and low learning curve.

CONS: If you wash it the wood grain can rise, causing future dough to stick.

BEST FOR: This pin is all-purpose.

PRICE RANGE: $5 to $40 depending on the wood and finish. I like maple, which is usually at around $10. J.K. Adams turns out a great maple pin from Vermont.

CARE: Wipe down with a wet towel or vinegar mixture after use. Sand lightly if someone accidentally left it sitting in water. Resist the urge to bop them with it.

ALTERNATIVES: If you prefer, you can get a dowel rolling pin. They are perfect wooden cylinders with a similar ease of use. If you're interested in getting consistent thicknesses, then this is the pin to get because you can put special-made rubber bands on the edges of the pin to achieve an even dough thickness. Joseph Joseph makes an adjustable rolling pin with all the bells and whistles for around $20.

Ravioli Rolling Pin

RECOMMENDED OR NOT: Only if you make ravioli more than four times a year.

PROS: This pin makes simple and lovely ravioli. If the pin and pasta are both well-floured, it rolls over the stuffed dough easily.

CONS: It can be easy to overstuff the pasta and have the filling squish out the sides. If pressure isn't applied to the middle of the pin as well as the handles, then some of the middle ravioli won't be sealed. It's also a one-purpose pin. The fine pieces of wood can break after a few years of heavy use. Difficult to clean.

BEST FOR: Rolling out ravioli. That is all.

PRICE RANGE: $20 to $40 depending on the wood and finish.

CARE: Keep this in a drawer not stuffed with too many other tools. Things can get caught in the holes or get stuck. Clean by brushing off the flour; do not soak!

Marble Rolling Pin

RECOMMENDED OR NOT: Only if you live in a hot climate with no AC and make only super delicate dough (like croissant or puff), otherwise pass.

PROS: These are very pretty and their natural weight does some of the work for you. They are naturally a few degrees below room temperature, which can give you a few precious extra moments to work with your dough. You can even chill a marble pin in the fridge before using it to get more time.

CONS: The super slick texture can promote the dough sticking and if it has handles, they'll face a lot of wear and tear from the heavy marble. They can also chip easily. Get one with a base so you don't end up with 5 pounds (2.3 kg) of marble rolling out of the cabinet onto your toes.

BEST FOR: Very temperature-sensitive dough.

PRICE RANGE: $16 to $40.

CARE: These can be washed in the sink, but do not put them in the dishwasher to avoid cracking or ruining the wooden handles.

Silicone Rolling Pin

RECOMMENDED OR NOT: Nope.

PROS: Uhh, it comes in pretty colors? Not a reason to buy something!

CONS: Water can get under the silicone sheath. They work great the first and second time, but for longevity I haven't found one I really like. The more you use them the greasier they can feel even with thorough cleaning.

BEST FOR: Re-gifting.

PRICE RANGE: $20 to $40.

CARE: Hand wash with soapy water.

Etched Rolling Pin

RECOMMENDED OR NOT: Yes, but only as a supplemental rolling pin.

PROS: An easy way to add extra decoration to your doughs. You can even order versions with your monogram or logo.

CONS: I hope you like the design because these guys aren't cheap. Dough can get stuck in the engravings. You'll need to do any preliminary rolling with another pin and use this just for the last pass.

BEST FOR: Rolled cookies, pie dough or savory dishes topped with puff pastry.

PRICE RANGE: $20 to $75 depending on the design. They come in acrylic and wood.

CARE: Be sure to have a brush on-hand to clear out any accumulated flour or dough that would disrupt the design.

Pasta Machine (I call mine Earl)

RECOMMENDED OR NOT: Yes! If you make fresh pasta, you aren't going to want any other kind. Can you make fresh pasta without a pasta machine? Yes, it's a pain but it's doable. The machines come with spaghetti and fettuccini attachments that are a blast to use.

PROS: They are super fun to use! They make short work of a tough dough and if you're looking to get a noncook involved in dinner, this is a great gateway tool.

CONS: Storage. They are big and clunky and you need to make sure you have a surface you can clamp them to (they come with a clamp).

BEST FOR: Pasta or making gum paste sugar flowers if you're into that kind of thing.

PRICE RANGE: $40 to $180. The more expensive ones are attachments for KitchenAid stand mixers; the motor of the mixer does all the work and you just stand there passing the dough through. Good times, but pricey.

CARE: This is tricky, because there is a lot of rustable metal here. I've had to wash mine once or twice. Your best bet is to wipe it down with a wet towel and then dry it with a paper towel. I store mine wrapped in plastic wrap so I don't introduce dust into whatever I'm making next. Stop asking me to introduce you, Dust! Nobody wants to hang out with you!

The Winner!

My favorite is the wooden tapered French rolling pin, because it can be used for almost everything you need to roll and, in a pinch, self-defense. Thwack!

Other Tools of the Trade

METAL BOWL: You can use glass or porcelain, but a metal bowl is more likely to be below room temperature, thus keeping whatever you're mixing cool. Gather a kitchen towel underneath it to keep it from sliding around the counter.

PIE DISH: I prefer a glass pie dish in most cases. A dark gray nonstick pie tin will absorb too much heat and overcook the crust while undercooking the filling. With a glass dish, you can see exactly how well done the crust is. If the dough is looking super pale but the top is browning too aggressively, you can cover the top with foil to stop the browning and continue to cook the dish until it's how you like it; this works for most pies too. A glass Pyrex dish should run you about $8, so it's not a total tragedy when you leave it at your friend's house.

MICROPLANE: This all-purpose grater was originally a wood rasp. It can take the edges off a wooden block (so watch your fingertips!). It's perfect for zesting citrus and grating garlic, nutmeg, chocolate, ginger and cheese. Just grate the dry ingredient first and clean it in between tasks. If yours comes with a plastic shield, you can slide it on backward to catch whatever you're grating, which is especially useful for nutmeg and chocolate, two things that react to static electricity and will magically coat everything nearby. They are around $12 and a must-have for every kitchen. It's worth it to buy two and it is the perfect shape to be a stocking stuffer, just leave the cover on. Ouch!

SPIDER: This long-handled wire disk is perfect for the retrieval of ravioli, dumplings and blanched veggies. They are about $10 and worth every penny. The ones with the bamboo handles look nice but they tend to fall apart too fast for my liking. My all-metal spider was $15 and has lasted me quite a while and still looks great.

PASTRY BLENDER: This handheld device with three to five curved blades will make you feel like Wolverine, if Wolverine were a baker. And at only $5 to $10, it's a deal. Alternatively, you can use a cheap, plastic bowl scraper, which is usually around $2. The scraper is rectangular and curved on one side to efficiently scrape out your bowl. Either will make short work of cut-in doughs.

BENCH SCRAPER: Total must-have. They are around $5 and some even have a ruler printed on the side. I have three of varying lengths that I use to portion dough, scrape up chopped veggies and herbs and even to get a perfect edge on the side of a cake (you hold it sideways and keep it flush with the turntable as you spin the cake around). Don't try to scrape things up with your knife! It dulls the blade and will slice your hand, not to mention the sound is like nails on a chalkboard. If you simply must use your knife, be sure to flip it over and use the back to keep the edge intact.

PLASTIC WRAP OR PARCHMENT PAPER: If you form your completed dough into a disk, it will have a larger surface area and cool faster. It will also be easier to roll out into a circle. Store it wrapped in plastic wrap and if you have a vexing surface to roll on, place your dough disk between two sheets of parchment paper and roll your dough to its desired shape. Chill before attempting to peel the paper back!

Tips for the Best Ingredients

For having just a few ingredients, dough is a pretty complex thing. Understanding a few fundamentals will educate your technique.

Flour

CAKE AND PASTRY FLOURS: These have a lower protein content, meaning they contain less gluten, giving them a more delicate crust. Think cakey, not crispy.

ALL-PURPOSE AND BREAD FLOURS: These are higher in gluten. Think pizza dough, pasta and baguettes.

HOW TO MEASURE FLOUR: Always transfer your flour from the bag to another container to aerate it. It has probably traveled across the country to get to you with literal tons of flour on top of it. You'll get the most accurate volume measurement from fluffed flour. A cup of flour scraped out of a packed bag could actually be a cup and a half if it isn't fluffed up. King Arthur Flour is my all-around favorite. It has been around since 1790 and is a fully employee-owned company; even more important, they are passionate bakers consistently delivering a superior product.

HOW TO FLOUR YOUR SURFACE: Use a sifter or a shaker, or hold a handful of flour in your hand and shake it like dice. When you're kneading dough, you want as little flour as possible to avoid offsetting the recipe, but go for the flour when you're rolling because you *do not* want that baby to stick to the counter! You can always brush off any excess; flour not mixed into anything and cooked just tastes bitter and sad.

Salt

If you forget salt, the dough will taste a bit flat and stale.

KOSHER SALT: I prefer kosher salt for almost everything I make, whether sweet or savory. Kosher refers to the size of the crystals. It's the salt that's packed onto a kosher slaughtered animal to draw out impurities. Remember this if you ever buy a kosher chicken or turkey! They've already been salted.

TABLE SALT: Table salt is too fine: the crystals are much smaller, so more salt will fit in the teaspoon, making things ultimately too salty. If your recipe calls for 1 teaspoon of salt but all you have is table salt, then reduce the amount to $^2/_3$ teaspoon or it will be too salty.

Butter

There is no industry standard for how much salt actually gets added to butter, so always use *unsalted butter* so you can control the amount of seasoning.

EUROPEAN-STYLE BUTTER: I like to use this butter because it has a higher fat percentage, resulting in a more tender final product.

CULTURED BUTTER: This butter is made with a soured cream that can have a slightly tangy flavor. It is great for toast, but the expense and flavor impact rule it out for baking with me. Butter actually coats the strands of gluten, keeping them short and hindering their development, which keeps your baked goods tender and not chewy like a baguette.

BUTTER TEMPERATURE: The temperature of the butter is incredibly important. If you are hoping to *cream* the butter, then it needs to be at room temperature. If your room is cold, then feel free to microwave for 10 seconds or, my favorite, flash a blowtorch over the mixing bowl as it spins a few times. You can also fill a large glass jar with boiling water, let it sit for 1 minute, pour it out and then invert it over the stick of butter. It's just hot enough to make it go soft but not melty. That jar is *hot* though, so use an oven mitt. Or if you are practicing the "cut-in butter" method, then you'll want to be sure your butter is straight-from-the-refrigerator cold so that it doesn't melt and disappear into the flour. The small pellets of butter will then melt during the cooking process and leave tiny pockets behind. These pockets become flakes, and we love them and end up wearing them.

Sugar

A *triangle* is the common lingo for sugar in the pastry biz. Some of the sugar in dough will melt during mixing, and some won't. The sugars that do melt will coat the gluten, making it even more tender. The crystals that don't melt during mixing will melt during baking, causing the product to spread. This is why your chocolate chip cookies on one day may be thick and the next day spread too far—it has to do with how long you mixed the butter and sugar.

GRANULATED SUGAR: Unless it's specified in the recipe, "sugar" means granulated sugar. It's our "all-purpose" sugar and the tiny crystals make creaming a breeze.

BROWN SUGAR: Brown sugar is just granulated sugar with some of the molasses that was extracted during the refinement process added back to it. This extra moisture is what sends it into brick territory the day after we open it. Store it in an airtight container with some mini-marshmallows to keep it workable for a longer period of time. The added moisture in brown sugar will also promote spreading, which is why most chocolate chip cookies call for a combination of brown and granulated sugar. You get the best of both worlds.

POWDERED (OR CONFECTIONERS') SUGAR: Powdered sugar is just regular sugar that's been pulverized to dust. A small amount of cornstarch is added in to keep it loose. It's not great for the creaming method but is great for making baked goods tender and sweet. In a pinch, you can absolutely make your own if you have a high-powered blender.

Water

Cold water keeps the butter cold and hydrates the flour juuuuuust enough to come together. I fill up a Pyrex measuring cup with ice water and sprinkle it with my fingers, holding in the ice. No, this is not an exact measurement, so add a little at a time and trust yourself.

The Best Techniques for Rolling Out Dough

Watching someone roll a perfect circle of dough is a Zen experience. They expertly apply just the right amount of pressure to create a symmetrical disk of even thickness that easily comes away from the rolling surface. This doesn't happen your first time. Your first crust may have looked like a Rorschach test and gotten stuck to the table, leaving blobs behind. Practice, practice, then practice some more. This will all become muscle memory. Here are some tips to follow to make it as easy as possible.

Rest the Dough

First things first: did you rest your dough? Those gluten strands got a workout when you made the dough, and they need to relax back down before you roll or it will snap right back, never giving you the shape you want and/or it will shrink drastically in the oven! Make sure it has chilled for at least 30 minutes.

Start in the Center

Place your chilled disk on a floured surface. Begin in the middle, making short rolling movements. Is it cracking? Don't freak out! It will be okay. Go drink a glass of water; it will give the dough a minute to warm up just a touch and you're probably not drinking enough water anyway. Move the dough after every two or three rolls to make sure it isn't sticking and rotate it a quarter turn. As you twist it, pick up a bit more of the scattered flour to keep the next roll from sticking too. If you need more flour, add more flour. You can always brush away excess flour when you're done, which is a lot easier than prying soft stuck-on dough from your counter. Repeat the process, never rolling the pin over and off the edges. If you do that, it will make the edges too thin and screw up your shape. Is it still sticking to the counter? Gently slide an offset spatula underneath to get it up with the least amount of damage. Transfer the dough by rolling it up onto the pin from the top down and then unfurl it, rolling away from you from the bottom up, onto a dish or piece of parchment to chill.

Roll on the Right Surface

You want to roll on a smooth, dry surface. Marble is lovely because, like metal, its natural state is below room temperature, giving you more time to roll. You can buy a good-sized marble slab for around $60 from Sur La Table if your counters just won't cut it. I also really like wooden tables. The nap of the wood naturally grabs onto the dough so it doesn't slide around, and that's especially great for kneading dough.

Pâte Brisée

This simple and delicious dough is my go-to dough and perfect for both sweet and savory applications. It's flaky and not too sweet, so you can use it for both quiches and tarts. Because there are no eggs or dairy, it keeps longer than other doughs in the freezer (months!) or fridge (a week). But alas, because there are no eggs or dairy, it can be trickier to work with, and less moisture means less gluten development. It can look crumbly and dry at first. Trust in yourself and the dough. A few dry-looking spots will hydrate as it chills. If it's "falling apart" crumbly, you can sprinkle a few drops of cold water on it until it comes together. The technique we're using here is the cut-in method of introducing butter to our dough. You'll just need some flour and a pin to roll it out.

MAKES: One 8-inch (20-cm) tart shell (double the recipe to get a top and a bottom)

1½ cups (150 g) all-purpose flour

¼ tsp salt

Pinch of sugar

8 tbsp (115 g) butter

4–5 tbsp (60-75 ml) ice cold water, divided

Troubleshooting Pâte Brisée: Because it's so flaky, the dough can crack when you blind bake it (baking it before filling it). If this happens, simply reserve any scraps of dough you had and smear a small bit onto the crack to prevent your filling from spilling out and either sticking to the pie dish or cookie sheet it's on. If you are filling it with something that needs no further baking, like a lemon curd or chocolate ganache, brush some melted white or dark chocolate over that crack to keep it from leaking and making a mess.

Whisk the flour, salt and sugar together in a cool metal bowl. Whisking aerates the flour enough, so there is no need to sift it.

Cut the cold butter into ¼-inch (6-mm) cubes and add to the flour mixture. Rock your bowl scraper or pastry blender back and forth over the flour and butter mixture to "cut" the butter pieces into the flour.

When your butter pieces are the size of lentils, begin sprinkling the cold water over the mixture. If you forgot what a lentil looks like, it's about half the size of a pea. If you forgot what a pea looks like, I want you to eat more vegetables.

Continue to work the mixture with the bowl scraper, a fork or your fingers just enough to make it start to come together into a mass. The less you work the dough, the more tender it will be. Flour can be moody! Some days it wants all the water, some days not so much. Add 2 to 3 tablespoons (30 to 45 ml) at first and mix in; if it's still dry, and it likely will be, then add the rest. It's normal to have a few crumbs left on the bottom. If it's not coming together at all, then go ahead and sprinkle on another teaspoon of water. You should be able to grip a handful in your palm and have it keep its shape without crumbling away.

Turn the dough out onto a clean surface and smoosh the dough in small increments with the heel of your hand, pushing it forward. The fancy word for this is *fraisage*. Scrape it all up and form it into a disk to chill for at least half an hour. We need the butter to cool back down and the gluten to relax.

If you're in a serious time pinch, it is possible to mix the flour and butter in a stand mixture until it's lentil-sized and then add the ice water and pulse your mixer just until it's combined. It might not be as tender, but it gets the job done for sure.

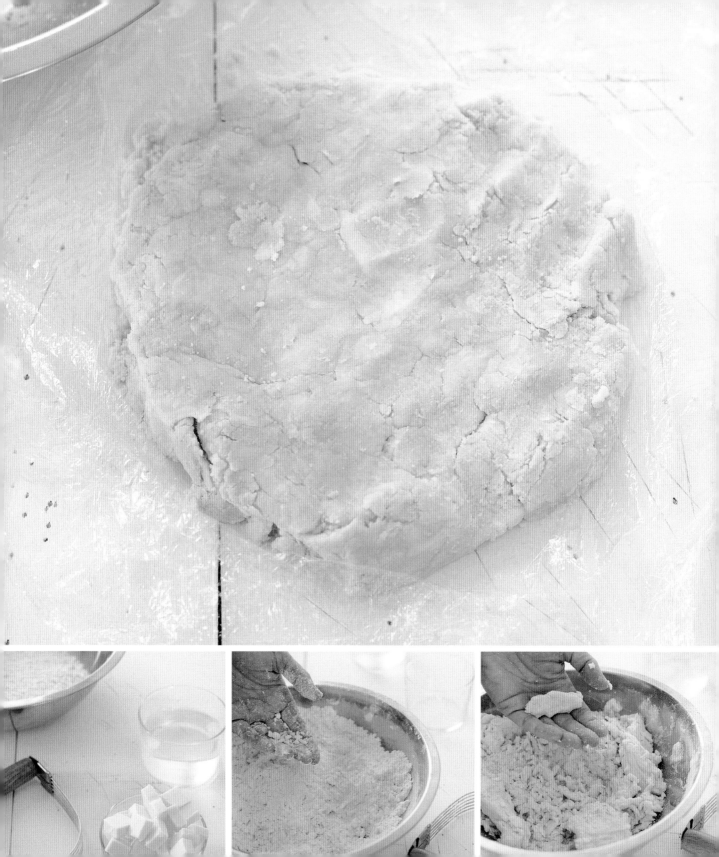

Prime Time Fruit Galette

We've all been there. We need dessert and all we have left are some past-their-prime peaches, plums or cherries (frozen is fine too!). Those babies are just begging to be reborn in galette form. I'm not sure, but I think galette is French for "no it's not perfect, it's rustic!" It's the same technique as making a pie but without the pie dish. I recommend using a sheet pan with raised sides in case any juice tries to escape.

MAKES: One 9-inch (23-cm) galette

1 recipe Pâte Brisée (page 18)

3 cups (450 g) ¼" (6-mm) slices stone fruit

½ cup plus 2 tbsp (120 g) sugar, divided

Pinch of salt

Zest of 1 lemon

1 tbsp (15 ml) lemon juice

3–4 tbsp (28–38 g) cornstarch

1 tbsp (15 ml) milk

Preheat the oven to 400°F (205°C). Line a sheet pan with parchment paper.

Roll the chilled pâte brisée into a 12-inch (30-cm) round and place on the prepared sheet pan.

In a bowl, toss the fruit with ½ cup (95 g) of the sugar, salt, lemon zest, lemon juice and cornstarch. Pile the fruit in the center of the dough, leaving an edge of about 2 inches (5 cm). Fold the dough over the fruit, pleating it as you go. It's up to you how much fruit you would like to leave exposed, but covering more of it will keep a lot of the moisture in and give you a yummier crust to eat. Brush the outside of the crust with milk and sprinkle generously with the remaining 2 tablespoons (25 g) of sugar. Bake for 30 to 40 minutes, until the crust is golden brown. Cool and serve warm or at room temperature.

Note: If your fruit is super juicy, toss the sliced pieces in the sugar mixture and let it sit in a strainer for 20 minutes, then add the cornstarch and pile on the galette dough. Sugar is hygroscopic, which means it absorbs moisture. As it sits with the fruit, it will pull moisture from it to drain through the strainer. Feel free to add this sweet fruit water to seltzer.

Quick Puff Pastry

So flaky, so versatile … so easy? Yup! This version of puff pastry takes a lot of the steps out. You see, puff pastry and croissants are what we call "laminated dough." There are layers upon layers of butter and dough. When the product hits the heat of the oven, the butter melts and leaves behind a pocket, a flake if you will. We keep a lot of the layers in this dough, but we're just less precious about keeping each layer complete from edge to edge.

MAKES: 2 sheets or enough for 40 pigs in blankets

1 ⅔ cups (165 g) all-purpose flour

1 tsp salt

2 tbsp (30 g) cold butter, squished to make it pliable

⅔ cup (160 ml) ice water

1 cup (227 g) super cold butter, cut into ½" (13-mm) cubes

Troubleshooting Puff Pastry

If you're working in a warm environment, you'll find that the butter starts to liquefy and you lose all your precious layers. Don't be afraid to keep sticking the dough back in the freezer for 5 to 10 minutes. Your patience will pay off with thousands of delicious flakes.

If the dough keeps springing back on you, then give it a rest—the dough that is. The gluten needs a moment to relax before you get it to its full length.

Add the flour, salt and pliable cold butter to the bowl of a stand mixer fitted with the paddle attachment and mix on low speed. With the mixer running on low, slowly stream in enough of the cold water until a dough starts to form.

As the mixer continues to run, add all of the super cold butter chunks and mix just until all of the butter is mixed in. Turn the dough out onto a sheet of plastic wrap and form it into a flattish block and refrigerate for at least half an hour.

Roll the dough into a long rectangle about 12 x 18 inches (30 x 45 cm) and complete two book turns: fold up one quarter of the dough to nearly the middle and then fold the top quarter down to nearly the middle and then close it like a book, then give it a quarter turn and repeat. Chill the dough for 30 minutes.

Repeat two more book turns and you're done. Let it rest for another 30 minutes in the refrigerator before using. It will keep in the refrigerator for 2 to 3 days or in the freezer for a couple months.

Remember not to roll over the farthest and nearest ends of the dough; you can flatten them out effectively by moving the dough 90 degrees. Letting the rolling pin pass over the edge will seal up edges and screw up your layers. Sticking to the counter? You can release it by shimmying an offset spatula below it and sprinkling more flour underneath. Don't be afraid to roll with a lot of flour, you can always get rid of the excess with a dry pastry brush before you fold or use it.

Pumped-Up Pigs in Blankets

Hey, remember that awesome quick puff pastry we just made? Well let's put it to use with some kicked-up pigs in blankets. The homemade puff pastry is all butter, as opposed to a lot of store-bought brands, which have hydrogenated oils instead. It's like the difference between some scratchy, weird airplane blanket and something soft and sweet Grammom knit you. If you do go with store-bought, make sure it's all butter.

MAKES: 20 pieces

1 egg

Pinch of salt

1 recipe Quick Puff Pastry (page 22)

¼ cup (40 g) crumbled membrillo (quince paste)

⅓ cup (40 g) grated manchego cheese

2 lb (900 g) fully cooked Spanish chorizo sausage, cut into 2½" (6.3-cm) pieces

Preheat the oven to 400°F (205°C). Line two cookie sheets with parchment paper.

In a bowl, beat the egg with a pinch of salt until totally liquefied and set aside.

Roll the puff pastry into two 8 x 12-inch (20 x 30-cm) rectangles on a floured surface and spread the crumbled membrillo paste on top. Sprinkle the manchego over the membrillo.

Cut each piece of pastry in half lengthwise so they are 4 x 12 inches (10 x 30 cm). Line a row of the sausage along either the tops or bottoms of each sheet. Roll the pastry over the sausage first, and then over the cheese and membrillo. Seal the edges with a brush of egg wash and slice into 2-inch (5-cm) logs. Place the rolls on the prepared baking sheet 2 inches (5 cm) apart from one another.

Chill for 10 to 15 minutes to reset the butter and then bake until puffed up and golden brown, about 25 to 30 minutes.

Note: If you can't find membrillo paste, you can spread a thin layer of apricot jam. After they are assembled, these may be frozen for up to a month.

Homemade Pasta Dough

Forget the boxed stuff! Unless the pasta is a tube or a curly shape, making your own fresh pasta dough is where it's at! If you can find Italian "00" flour, use it to make very delicate, yet chewy pasta. If not, all-purpose or bread flour both work really well. Because the all-purpose flour has less gluten, you'll need to knead it a bit more. No matter what, though, it'll be better than the dry pasta in the pantry. The pasta machine is optional but it really is a big timesaver. Make it once without the machine to see how much you love fresh pasta and then let everyone know you want one for Christmas. Make sure you use fine sea salt, as coarse crystals will tear the dough.

SERVES: 4

2½ cups (250 g) Italian-style "00," bread or unbleached all-purpose flour, plus more for rolling

1 tsp fine sea salt

4 large eggs, beaten

1 tbsp (15 ml) extra-virgin olive oil

Semolina, for finishing (optional)

Place the flour and salt in a large mixing bowl and whisk to combine. Form a well in the center of the flour mixture and pour in the eggs and oil. Using your hand or a wooden spoon, swirl the eggs into the flour mixture, working from the inside out.

When the pasta dough is thoroughly mixed, turn it out onto a floured table. The Italians prefer to use a wooden table because it sort of grips the dough. You can also do this on a wooden cutting board for ease of cleanup.

Knead the dough until it is smooth and flexible but not sticky; if it is sticky, try adding small amounts of flour until it no longer sticks to your hands or the table. A little sticky is okay, but if it is so wet or sticky that when you lightly touch it some dough comes off on you, it is too wet and sticky. In that case, add 1 tablespoon (6 g) more of flour and continue to knead. It will take about 5 minutes.

Shape the dough into a ball and flatten into a disk. Cover with plastic wrap and allow the dough to rest for at least 20 minutes. The gluten is wide awake right now and raring to snap back; resting will relax it so you can roll it out.

If you're using a pasta machine, then clamp it to a table. Divide the dough into thirds. If you do it all at once the final roll will end up being 5-foot (1.5-m)-long pieces of pasta, fun to look at but *no bueno*. Keep the dough you aren't currently working with covered in plastic wrap to keep it from drying out.

(continued)

Homemade Pasta Dough (Cont.)

Press the dough down to about ¼-inch (6-mm) thickness so that it will fit inside the widest setting of the pasta machine. Pass the dough through the machine, catching it with one hand as you roll with the other; this is a good time to involve your kids, spouse, letter carrier, etc. Take the dough and trifold it like a letter. Turn the dough so the S-seamed end faces the rollers and send it through on the widest setting again. Fold, turn and roll once more on the widest setting. If it looks very shaggy, repeat the process 2 to 3 more times. Now your pasta should have reached optimum springiness and anything that wasn't perfectly mixed together now is.

Continue rolling the pasta through the machine without folding, adjusting the roller size to a smaller setting after each pass, until the desired thickness is reached. Depending on the make and model of your machine, the numbers will go up or down. You'll likely need to pull the handle out as you adjust it to change the thickness. If the pasta sheet becomes too large to handle, cut it into more manageable lengths and continue rolling. The bench scraper is perfect for that.

If you want to make spaghetti, linguini or fettuccini, most pasta machines come with an attachment that hooks onto the top of the machine. The hand crank comes out of the main rollers and fits easily into the noodle die section. Feed the pasta sheets through just as you would the regular pasta roller and watch as real live noodles come out the other end. Toss them with plenty of flour so they don't stick together. The flour will just come off in the pasta water. If you would like to make pappardelle, roll the sheets up into a tube and cut by hand with a sharp knife.

Set aside, covered with a clean kitchen towel, and be gentle with the finished pasta; if you press the pieces together, they will stick. The pasta can be cooked immediately or covered with plastic wrap and refrigerated for up to 24 hours before use. Fresh pasta only takes about 3 minutes to cook in boiling salted water.

Troubleshooting Pasta Dough: Often the dough is either too dry or too wet; eggs vary greatly in size and the flour takes time to absorb the moisture. If you rush it, it will feel dry at first and then too wet and sticky to use. It's better to have the dough be a little too dry than wet. Wet sticks to everything. You, the pin, a pasta machine, everything. When you're mixing the dough, if there is more than a teaspoon of flour crumbs refusing to join the dough mass, sprinkle them with ¼ teaspoon of water and continue to knead it until it's completely absorbed. If the dough is just over the top wet and is coming off on your hands, first rub your hands together like you're coming up with an evil plan—this will get everything off and back onto the dough, as opposed to your sink drain where it will clog and be gross. Second, add 1 tablespoon (6 g) of flour to the top and another underneath the dough. You should be able to incorporate the flour. Keep adding and kneading in small increments until the dough is sticky but no longer coming off on you. The more you knead it, the smoother and less sticky it will get. It's always better to try kneading a bit more first than automatically reaching for backup flour.

Lemon Ricotta Ravioli with Sage Brown Butter Sauce

Sure, ravioli are delicious, but they are also fantastic at cleaning out the fridge! Leftover omelet filling? Chop it up and put it in. Tiny nub of cheese in there? In it goes. I'm usually only cooking for three, so a pack of sausages means I always have one left over. Yup, you guessed it, chop it up and fill some ravioli.

It's okay to have a plan, too, though, and this decadent lemon ricotta cheese ravioli is sure to impress. Browning the butter adds an entire dimension to the flavor profile. Don't just save it for this sauce; try it everywhere and then keep some in the fridge for cookies.

SERVES: 4

FILLING

1¼ cups (155 g) ricotta cheese

Zest of 2 lemons

2 tbsp (22 g) freshly grated Parmesan cheese

1 egg yolk (save the white to seal the ravioli)

½ tsp salt

1 tbsp (15 ml) heavy cream

RAVIOLI

1 recipe Homemade Pasta Dough (page 26)

1 egg white, beaten

To make the filling, in a bowl, smoosh all of the ingredients together with the side of a spatula until homogenous. Cover and chill until ready to fill the ravioli.

To make the ravioli, there are a few ways to fill them. First, you'll need sheets of pasta. Ideally, you'll use your trusty, not rusty, pasta machine or stand mixer pasta attachment. Don't have one? You can still play along, but you'll just need to work those arms a bit. Roll the dough until it's about ¹⁄₁₆ inch (1.5 mm) thick—not so thin you can read type through it but almost. It needs to hold in our filling. If you want to err on the side of thicker the first few times, then go for it.

Next you can cut squares or use a ravioli cutter or a ravioli tray. No matter what method you use, the key is to not overfill. For a 3-inch (7.6-cm)-wide ravioli, you'll only need about 2 teaspoons (10 g) of filling.

Wet the sides with a brush (or finger) dipped in the reserved egg white and then press to seal the top on.

It's ready to be dropped into some boiling water. Water that's juuuuust boiling. A big rolling boil will be too much of a ruckus for our delicate ravioli. When the ravioli are cooked, they'll pop up to the top. This should take 3 to 5 minutes. Draining into a colander is too aggressive. Better to gently lift them out with a spider.

(continued)

Lemon Ricotta Ravioli
with Sage Brown Butter Sauce (Cont.)

SAGE BROWN BUTTER SAUCE

6 tbsp (86 g) unsalted butter

8–10 fresh sage leaves, cut into chiffonade

Freshly grated Parmesan cheese, for garnish

Freshly ground pepper

2 tbsp (30 ml) lemon juice (it's easier to zest the lemon first and then juice it)

Zest of 1 lemon

To make the sauce, melt the butter in a shallow saucepan over medium-high heat. After the bubbles begin to subside, start swirling the butter or stirring it with a silicone spatula. The milk solids will begin to toast on the bottom of the pan. Continue to swirl until the butter takes on a golden hue. It will fill the kitchen with the smell of roasted hazelnuts, which is why it's called *beurre noisette* in French (hazelnut butter).

Drop the chiffonaded sage (multiple leaves rolled up lengthwise and then cut into thin strips) into the butter and let sizzle for about 30 seconds.

Lower the ravioli into the sauce, swirl around to coat and then serve with a sprinkling of Parmesan, freshly ground pepper, a few squirts of lemon juice and a dusting of lemon zest.

Chapter 2

Sheet Pan Handling

The Surfaces We Bake On

We may already know that heat turns the fast-moving molecules of water into steam, but what does it do to a sheet of metal? When metal is exposed to heat it actually expands, and if your pan is too thin or your oven is unevenly heating, you're likely to hear a loud bang and open the door to find a warped pan. Ever put a hot pan on a metal table? It can sound like a gunshot when the table buckles. The good news is the metal will usually go back to being sort of flat afterward. The bad news is it may have launched whatever you were baking loose into the oven and given you a heart attack.

Every time it happens it stresses the metal. Eventually, it will crack or warp beyond usability. If you're in the market for a sheet pan, you'll want to go for a thicker cookie sheet. If the packaging loudly touts "rolled edges," then that likely means that the metal is very thin—the edges have to be rolled or else it's razor sharp and will slice the heck out of anyone who comes near it. Possibly the coolest Bond weapon available but crummy when you're the one reaching for it.

The Best Materials for the Job

Aluminum

RECOMMENDED OR NOT: For baking, yes. Read the label! You'll want them to be reinforced with galvanized steel to prevent them from warping at higher temperatures.

PROS: Usually fairly cheap. Decent heat conduction.

CONS: Aluminum can react with acid. Roasted tomatoes end up tasting weirdly metallic. You can avoid this by cooking on a sheet of parchment paper.

PRICE RANGE: $10 to $20.

Let's Talk about Hot Spots

All ovens have hot spots: it's just a fact of life and you shouldn't feel bad about it. Some of my favorite ovens have hot spots. Still, they can wreak havoc on your food. Want to find out if you have hot spots that are screwing up your food? Preheat your oven to 350°F (177°C) and roll out some dough. It doesn't matter what kind. Honestly, use a tube of crack-apart crescent rolls if you want—this isn't for eating, it's for hot spot finding. Cover the entire area of your largest sheet pan and pop it in the oven until it's all baked. Check it every 10 minutes until it's golden brown. When it's cool, flip it out and you'll see the proof right there. Are there areas that got waaaaay too much color? Or is it pretty uniform? If you're lucky and it's all uniformly baked, then no need to rotate things as you bake them. Have some definite areas of "got baked more"? Then you'll want to always be sure to rotate your baked goods while they're cooking. For cookies that take 10 minutes, just rotating them once at 5 minutes should do the trick. For something like bread or roasted potatoes, you'll want to rotate every 15 minutes or so. Is half of it burnt to a crisp and the other half completely raw? Something in your oven isn't working and you'll need to get a pro out to take a peek.

Black Steel

RECOMMENDED OR NOT: No. While they're great at getting hot, I usually find the surface is just too dark to cook delicate things on.

PROS: Very nonstick (cookies will slide right off) and they're great heat conductors.

CONS: Super heavy and a bit more expensive. Because they are so dark, they absorb more heat. This results in a darker bottom to whatever you're baking. Ever pull out what look like pale, beautiful cookies but they are scorched on the bottom? Your pan is probably too dark. They are also fussy and will rust if you don't clean and dry them right away, which is tricky because they can take a while to cool down. If you have these, I recommend lowering your oven temperature by about 25°F (14°C) to keep from having a charred bottom (tee hee).

PRICE RANGE: $20 to $30.

Insulated

RECOMMENDED OR NOT: Yes if you bake lots of fussy macarons or other low-temperature items. There's a cushion of air between the two aluminum layers.

PROS: This means they are slower to heat up and brown if you love making delicate cookies that shouldn't have color, like macarons or sugar cookies.

CONS: Less heat absorption means a slower cooking time. They also usually don't have higher edges, so you can only use them for nonjuicy endeavors. Slightly more expensive.

PRICE RANGE: Around $25.

Nonstick

RECOMMENDED OR NOT: No.

PROS: Your burnt cookies slide off.

CONS: Hmm, a nonstick surface is not usually something you want to heat up in an oven. Teflon and the fumes it releases when heated have been linked to some scary things. I'm not a Teflon scientist, so I'm just going to say avoid. There are a lot of PFOA-free alternatives out there but they tend to be very dark, giving you the same "too dark = too much heat" problem from the black steel cookie sheet. If you're having a problem with overly sticky things, you're better off using some parchment paper to line your pan. If your cookies are still sticking, wait until they are cool enough to touch and then peel the paper off of the cookie instead of the cookie off the paper.

PRICE RANGE: $15 to $35.

CARE: Even with hand washing, these sheets can get stained and pretty sad looking after years of use. Oils and nonstick cooking sprays polymerize around 400°F to 500°F (205°C to 260°C), meaning they become solid and glom onto the pan. This is actually what we do to our cast iron that makes it nonstick, but on cookie sheets it makes them look stained and can overly darken the sheet pan.

I love Bar Keepers Friend. Just wet the offending pan, sprinkle on some Bar Keepers Friend and then scour using a mildly abrasive sponge. Another great way to clean them is with a paste made from baking soda and hydrogen peroxide. In a small bowl, add enough peroxide to 1 cup (205 g) of baking soda to make a paste. Smear the paste onto the offending cookie sheet and let it set for 5 to 10 minutes. All your baked-on goop should wash right off. Smear off a test spot first and if it's still not budging, just give it more time. *Do not dishwash!* The soaps can cause the metal to pit and if it has a rolled edge, water can hang out in there and get rusty. Better off just hand washing.

Note: If it's listed, check out the number next to where it says stainless steel on the label or underside of your cookie sheet. If you see the numbers 18/10, 18/8 and 18/0, this is referring to the amount of chromium (first number, shiny hard metal, high temperature range) and nickel (second number, shiny but melts at a lower temperature) in your sheet. These are the most common food-grade steels. Steel is made by heating up iron with carbon and then adding these elements. It's a bit more complicated than that, but you get the gist. The 18/8 is the ideal number. Slightly less nickel, stronger pan, still resistant to corrosion. The 18/0 is just steel and chromium. It's still really good; you'll just have to take better care of it because it is more prone to rust. You should totally bring this up at your next cocktail party! Nerds unite!

The Winner!

I love the Nordic Ware Commercial sheet pans. For home use, the half sheet pans are perfect and you can get one for around $15. The jelly roll size is small enough that you can probably fit two on each rack side by side. I use them for almost everything that goes in my oven. I line them with parchment for cookies and leave them bare for roasted potatoes to get that extra layer of caramelization on the bottom. I also recommend purchasing a Silpat or two to fit inside the pan for extra-sticky projects and a cooling rack that fits inside as well for things like, oh, candied bacon. Also, placing the pan with a Silpat on it on the rack under your bubbling lasagna or overstuffed apple pie to catch overflow will make oven cleanup a lot easier! Always hand wash.

Other Tools of the Trade

PIZZA STONE/STEEL: Do you reeeeeeeeally need a pizza stone? Well, if you want to make great pizza, the answer is a resounding yes! These pizza platforms go into your oven before it's preheated. They even out the oven's heat and cook things nice and evenly. Your sheet pans shouldn't really go above 450°F (232°C) and we will want our ovens up in the range of 500°F (260°C) or more for pizza, so just flipping over a sheet pan isn't a great solve.

Did you do that experiment earlier where you tested your oven for hot spots? If your results were alarming, then by all means get a stone or steel and just leave it in the oven. You can put sheet trays right on top of it and it will help regulate the heat of the oven, resulting in more evenly baked goodies.

Don't get them wet! Stones are going to get stained, that's just a fact. If cheese or sauce bubbles over the side of the pizza onto the stone, the best you can do is scrape it off after it's cooled or wait until the offending toppings are reduced to ashes and brush them off. What makes the stone so great is that it absorbs moisture from the dough, resulting in a great crispy crust. If it absorbs too much moisture, say from washing it or letting sauce bubble off the pizza, it will crack. Sometimes spectacularly, sounding like a grenade went off in your oven. If it's just one big break, you can just push the stones back together and continue to use them but it's not pretty and makes moving them tricky. They run for around $20 to $60 or you can DIY using unglazed ceramic quarry tiles from your favorite big box store. Make sure that the stone doesn't cover the entire rack; you need room for airflow to properly cook. I use a giant cordierite slab from Sur La Table. It's around $60 and is large enough for two pizzas or a large sheet pan.

Newer to the market are steels. These are super-heavy, giant slabs of steel. These heat up super hot and bake off pizzas in short order. They are subject to rust, though, and weigh a ton, so figure it will probably live in your oven, which is cool with me if it is with you. Seriously, they are heavy! If you can order one with free shipping, it will save you the experience of watching it tear through your shopping bag or having to lurch from the store to your car.

If you have a cast-iron griddle, then just flip that baby over and pop it in the oven. It will work just as well as a steel. *Make sure the pizza you make isn't bigger than what you're cooking it on.*

PIZZA PEEL: These are super fun but not totally necessary. I find that beginning pizza makers have the hardest time getting a pizza to slide into the oven without snagging on the peel and launching all of the toppings onto the stone and creating a smoke cloud. The way around this is to use a lot of cornmeal, semolina or flour on the bottom of your pizza. Top the pizza when it is on the pizza peel, NOT on the countertop. You should be able to slide the pizza around on the peel; if not, it will definitely front flip into the oven. I use the one from American Metalcraft for around $10 from webstaurantstore.com, but most kitchen supply stores carry them. If you don't have one, then forming a pizza on a large cardboard cake circle and shimmying it onto your preferred cooking platform works too.

TONGS: Tongs are a nonnegotiable must-have. I use my tongs every darn day. If you make a lot of large roasts, you may want more than one set. Rösle makes some really beautiful tongs that magically lock when you close them upside down; this is great if storage is an issue. They carry a hefty price tag of around $30 per set. I also like the Oberhaus tongs with the business end being made out of silicone; they're much easier to clean up and they are about $10 for a two-pack. They'll lock shut by pulling the ring, which they can also hang from, and are a breeze to clean. Avoid the tongs that have a metal ring that flops around by the hinge to lock your tongs while not in use. They don't work well at locking and you'll feel like a spaz jerking the tongs around to dislodge the ring.

PASTRY BRUSH: I bought the most beautiful pastry brushes ever in Copenhagen. I hung them on my wall. I posted about them on Facebook. My friend Stephen commented that they looked like something from Home Depot. They were prettier than that, but he was right—they were essentially overpriced paintbrushes. And it turns out they are the worst. They've only been hand washed but the warping of the wood is ridiculous. When purchasing a pastry brush (sometimes called a basting brush), buy one with a lacquered handle. An untreated beechwood handle will warp and potentially mold. Winco has a great version for around $6. These have natural bristles and are glued in so do not dish-wash or wash with super-hot water, or the bristles will start to fall out, which can look disturbingly like human hair! Silicone brushes are okay but they don't absorb the egg wash or barbecue sauce, so they're a little trickier to use; on the other hand, they *can* be dish-washed and are much easier to clean. Still reasonable at $6 to $7 and up. I suggest getting one of each so you always have a dry one.

Tips for the Best Ingredients

"00" Flour

My preferred flour for making pizza dough is "00" caputo flour. The bag is super confusing, though. Sometimes there'll even be a picture of a cake on it, and you can NOT make pizza dough with cake flour. It also calls itself a "soft" flour. Rest assured that it has a substantial gluten content (12.5 percent!). The "00" refers to how finely it has been milled, and it has been milled finely. It feels like baby powder. This helps us make a dough with less water. I find it to be the easiest to work with and it gives the most consistently crispy crust.

Vanilla Extract

This is going to sound like sacrilege, so you should sit down. Sometimes it's okay to use imitation vanilla extract. I know, I know, it sounds insane but when something is baking at a high heat, all the nuances of flavor and smell bake off (just like with fancy olive oil). You're left with just the basic vanilla flavor that's the same as what you would get from an extract. Now, if you're making something that's not getting a lot of high heat or you're adding it after it's mostly cooked (pudding, for example), then by all means, break out the good stuff. For cookies, though, you're good to go with a bottle of much cheaper Sauer's Imitation Vanilla Extract. It's less than $3! Not too shabby when just one lonely vanilla bean will run you $4. For the real stuff, I like both McCormick and Nielsen-Massey; it just depends on how fancy the store is when I realize I need to buy more. They're both top-notch.

Lemon Zest

If you have a recipe calling for lemon juice and you're not also throwing in some zest, you're flushing extra flavor down the drain. I never skip this step; it's become muscle memory. If I'm holding a lemon, I'm automatically reaching for a microplane with my other hand. More often than not the lemon (or lime or orange) has a thin wax coating. It's an edible wax. It helps to keep the citrus fresh and pretty looking on its trip from somewhere warm to you. Still, I'd prefer not to eat it, it's not going to enhance any flavors. You can easily remove it by spraying it with a 50:50 vinegar to water solution, waiting 5 minutes and then scrubbing with a dish sponge under hot water. After the citrus is dried, it's good to go. If you're in a super rush, you can also grab the citrus in some metal tongs and run it over the flame of your gas oven for a few seconds. It's not as thorough, but I find it melts the wax off and I can just wipe them down after and use them right away. There is enough acid in the zest that it will burn through plastic! If you want to zest it before you're ready to use it, store it in the folds of some parchment paper. You'll lose some of the oil, but it keeps for an hour or two before getting weird.

Parmesan Cheese

A full wheel can be yours for the low, low price of $2,499 (Williams Sonoma). I have had the opportunity to cut apart and portion a few wheels and let me tell you, it's a tough job. I've seen two people go to the hospital trying to take one of these babies apart. They come in weighing about 80 pounds (36 kg). Have you ever been gifted a fancy set of cheese knives? Is one of them a funny little spade? That's for your Parm, baby! You wedge it in and twist, getting these delicious little nuggets. A nugget for the recipe and one to pop in your mouth.

Like Champagne, Parmesan can *only* be called by its name if it's from the regions of Parma and Reggio. If it's not called Parmigiano-Reggiano, then it's not! It can be tricky to tell in the United States. While the rest of the world abides by this labeling rule, the United States is still writing "Parmesan" on green canisters. Real Parm is made from cows that only feed from unmolested, nonchemically treated fields. The cheese is legally required to only contain milk, salt and rennet (an enzyme from animal intestines that causes milk to curdle—most cheese is made with animal rennet). All sorts of nonsense can happen with illegitimate Parm. The milk can be bleached, colors can be added, cellulose can be added to keep it granular—it's just not what you want. Spring for a chunk of actual Parmigiano-Reggiano. It should be embossed on the rind with the name written in a dot matrix. Make sure it doesn't look dried out, and it should be a bit oily. It will keep in the fridge for weeks. Buy it from a store that you know has a high cheese turnover. Those wheels are big; you don't want a hunk cut off of a wheel that's been sitting out too long. Store it in the fridge in a ziplock or a wax-lined cheese paper and break it off or grate it when you're ready to use it.

The Best Techniques for Sheet Pans

The humble sheet pan is my most reached-for kitchen tool. The low profile of its edges exposes it to all the heat the oven has to offer, quickly roasting or evenly baking in a short amount of time. Love a crispier brownie? Make them in a sheet pan. Do you like the toastier top of mac and cheese? Make it in a sheet pan. Muffin top aficionado? Heck, spread muffin batter into your sheet pan, top with some turbinado sugar and BOOM, you have a delicious tray of muffin top goodness waiting to be cut into cute bars. By cooking a thinner layer, your cook time will be greatly reduced. A 30-minute muffin at 350°F (163°C) will probably only take about 10 minutes, so keep an eye on it.

It's so all-purpose that unless you're roasting something giant and wet, a sheet pan is usually the way to go. They are incredibly versatile. And while yes, I give you some tips on how to clean them, don't be afraid of the dark marks. I love the look of a well-used sheet pan. As long as you give it a nice scrub, don't sweat the way it looks. The sheet pan is so versatile that genius food writer Melissa Clark recently came out with a cookbook dedicated to sheet pan dinners. Pick it up and store it next to this one.

Candied Bacon

Yes. Candied. Bacon. Feel free to get creative here! Want to add a little dried sage? Go for it. Some cayenne pepper? Yes, please! You'll need two sheet pans and some aluminum foil. This is a great party snack and it's best at room temperature, so make it an hour or two before people start to show up. And three words: Bloody Mary garnish. Be sure to use a rimmed aluminum baking sheet to keep any grease from spilling out.

MAKES: 1 pound (450 g)

½ cup (110 g) light brown sugar

1 tsp ground black pepper

½ tsp cayenne pepper

1 lb (450 g) thick-cut bacon

Preheat the oven to 325°F (163°C). Prepare a sheet pan with raised sides with a layer of aluminum foil.

Combine the sugar, pepper and cayenne in a bowl. Dredge the bacon slices in the sugar mixture to evenly coat and place on the foiled sheet. Sprinkle any remaining sugar mixture on top. Cover with a sheet of parchment paper and the second cookie sheet.

Bake in the oven for 30 minutes, or until your preferred level of crispiness has been reached. Carefully remove the sheet pan from the oven and cool until it stops bubbling. Peel the bacon up while it's still warm and plate (or else it will stick to the foil).

Slice-and-Bake Icebox Cookies

I use chopped cherries and walnuts in these cookies, but you can really use the base for almost anything. What's so great about this recipe is you can make the dough a month or two before you need the cookies and then just slice and bake off as you want them. It's great to have a log or two in the freezer during the holidays so you're always prepared. You'll need some parchment paper or plastic wrap on hand to make rolling them up a breeze. Adding the flour in increments will keep the cookies from developing too much gluten and getting tough.

MAKES: 40 cookies

¾ cup (172 g) butter, at room temperature

⅓ cup (64 g) sugar

¼ tsp salt

1½ cups (150 g) all-purpose flour

½ tsp vanilla extract (imitation is good)

Zest of 1 lemon

½ cup (58 g) chopped walnuts

⅓ cup (55 g) dried cherries, chopped

Add the butter and sugar to a large bowl or stand mixer bowl and beat on medium speed until light and fluffy.

Reduce the mixer speed and add the salt and flour in ¼-cup (25-g) increments. It doesn't have to be exact; you can eyeball it. Mix in the vanilla, zest, walnuts and cherries by hand.

Scrape approximately half of the dough onto a sheet of parchment or plastic wrap and form into a log about 1½ inches (4 cm) wide. Form into your desired shape, squared off or rolled into a circle, and chill in the refrigerator for at least 2 hours or up to a month in the freezer (let them sit in the refrigerator for a day, if possible, to make slicing easier).

Preheat the oven to 350°F (176°C). Line an aluminum rimmed or insulated cookie sheet with parchment.

Slice the logs into ¼-inch (6-mm) slices; you may need to reroll or keep moving the dough so the shape doesn't distort. Bake the cookies ½ inch (13 mm) apart for approximately 15 minutes or until the edges become golden brown. These cookies shouldn't take on too much color.

Pizza Dough

When I was fifteen, I started working in my boyfriend's mom's pizza restaurant. I ate pizza every single day and still would if I could. It is the most perfect food. The boyfriend is long gone but man, do I miss that pizza. Those were good times.

Use your pizza stone if you have one and having a plastic bowl scraper on hand will make life much easier too.

MAKES: Four 9-inch (23-cm) pizzas or two 14-inch (35-cm) pizzas

3½–4 cups (348–398 g) bread flour, plus more for rolling (all-purpose can be used in case of pizza emergency)

1 tsp sugar

1 envelope or 2¼ tsp (7 g) instant dry yeast (can be used interchangeably with active dry yeast—active dry yeast always needs to be dissolved in a liquid before use)

2 tsp (10 g) kosher salt

1½ cups (355 ml) water, 110°F (43°C)—warm but not hot to the touch

2 tbsp (30 ml) olive oil, plus more for the bowl

Combine all the ingredients in a large bowl and stir with a wooden spoon or by hand until the dough forms a ball. Or place the ingredients in a stand mixer with a dough hook or a food processor and mix until a dough forms. If the dough is sticky, add more flour, 1 tablespoon (6 g) at a time, until it comes together in a solid ball. If the dough is too dry, add more water, 1 teaspoon at a time.

Scrape the dough onto a lightly floured surface and gently knead into a smooth, firm ball, about 5 minutes.

Coat the inside of a large bowl with olive oil, add the dough, cover the bowl with plastic wrap and put it in a warm area to let it double in size, about 1 hour.

Turn the dough out onto a lightly floured surface and divide it into 2 equal pieces. Cover each with a clean kitchen towel or plastic wrap and let them rest for about an hour until they have doubled in size.

Pizza Party? Make the dough in advance and pop it into the fridge after it's been kneaded. It will proof slowly in the fridge and can be used within a day or two. This extra time can lend a yummy sourdough-like tang to the crust. Allow the dough to come to room temperature before forming it.

What's the Deal with Yeast?

Yeast are single-celled sugar-eating fungi. They burp out carbon dioxide and excrete alcohol. They are microscopic—it takes about 20 billion yeast cells to weigh just 1 gram! Instant yeast packets can be used interchangeably with active dry yeast—active dry yeast just always needs to be dissolved in a liquid before use; instant yeast can be put right into the recipe.

Margherita Pizza

Pizza goes waaaaay back in history. Ever since people have been smooshing grains together and slapping them on a hot surface, we've had flat breads. Peasants would top it with whatever they had on hand, usually cheap herbs, and bits of cheese or cured meats if they were lucky. The chef credited with the first Margherita pizza was Raffaele Esposito. He made it for the visiting King Umberto and Queen Margherita in the late 1800s. She, like any sane person, *loved* it, so he called it Pizza Margherita. The first known pizza shop was in Naples, Italy—and it's still there! The place is called Antica Pizzeria Port'Alba and it has a Yelp! rating of 4½ stars! *The first pizzeria ever has a Yelp! rating!* That just blows my mind. What's that half a star missing for? Centurions in the bathroom?

MAKES: Two 14-inch (35-cm) pizzas

Simple Pizza Sauce

2 large cloves garlic, crushed

1 tsp oregano (optional)

1 tbsp (15 ml) olive oil

1 (28-oz [794-g]) can crushed tomatoes

Salt and pepper

Pizza

1 recipe Pizza Dough (page 45)

1 lb (450 g) mozzarella, torn into small pieces (not soaking in water)

Torn basil leaves, to taste (Love basil? Pile it on. Hate it? Leave it off, this isn't rocket science.)

Preheat your oven to 500°F (260°C) with the stone or steel in it if using, allowing at least half an hour for your oven to preheat. This gives you time to prepare the sauce while you set out your dough to take the chill off.

To make the sauce, heat the garlic and oregano (if using) with the olive oil in a saucepan over medium heat. When the garlic starts to sizzle, add the tomatoes. With a wooden spoon, break apart the tomatoes. Simmer, uncovered, until the sauce is thick enough to mound on a spoon, about 15 minutes. Season to taste with salt and pepper.

To make the pizza, on a floured surface, press down on a dough ball to pop any giant gas bubbles. Stretch it into a circle with the palms of your hand, pressing down on the outer edges and tugging it. Starting in the middle will result in a too-thin crust. Continue until your desired size is met. Authentic Neapolitan pizza is not perfectly round! Feel free to scream that at anyone who isn't happy with your final shape. The key here is uniform thickness of dough and sometimes that means a less than perfect circle. Feeling ambitious? Well, then, after the first step of degassing the dough and a little stretching, you can tuck the back of your hands under opposing sides of the dough, 10:00 and 2:00 like on a steering wheel but with the backs of your fingers, being careful to keep your nails tucked under. Gently toss the dough into the air, making a bit of a spinning motion right before you release the dough. Practice this with your second pizza . . . just in case. And remember, at 500°F (260°C) no cooties can survive. Not that I'm condoning dough that's been on the floor, just sayin'.

(continued)

Margherita Pizza (Cont.)

Place your lovely circle of dough onto a pizza peel or parchment paper with a light dusting of flour or cornmeal. I can't stress this enough! After handling the dough you probably realized that even well-floured dough starts to feel sticky quickly and if you're pokey with your sauce and topping application, that baby will be stuck on the peel. Make life easier and liberally flour it or go with the parchment paper.

Top with ¼ cup (61 g) of sauce in the center and move it out in circles with the back of a spoon. Top with your mozzarella and bake for 8 to 12 minutes. Check it at 5! Commercial pizza ovens can go up to around 800°F (426°C), where they cook pies in about 3 minutes. Your oven is set to 500°F (260°C), but let's face it, do you trust your oven? Check it. It should have a golden brown crust and some dark brown or black spots on the cheese.

Slide the peel under your baked, bubbling pizza and shimmy it back out. Have a fork ready to aid the transfer if it's your first time. I like to move mine to a pretty, wooden cutting board so I don't have to move it again to serve. Let it cool down for a minute. The cheese needs to settle and congeal. After 3 or 4 minutes, you can artfully sprinkle your basil on top. Slice it and call me. I want some pizza too, please.

Notes: If you sauce your pizza with a sauce that's too wet, it will soak through the crust, resulting in a floppy slice. Don't let floppy slice happen to you.

You can use a can of whole tomatoes or crushed tomatoes, but not diced tomatoes. Diced tomatoes are treated with calcium chloride to keep their shape and will never break down; that's weird, skip them.

Cutting basil or soft herbs with a knife can cause it to oxidize (turn black) around the edges; roughly tear your leaves to keep them looking nice and fresh.

Feel free to use any other standard pizza toppings but note that meats should either be cured like pepperoni or precooked, like buffalo chicken.

Troubleshooting Pizza

Total disaster? Some people just have a really hard time getting this down. No worries. You can always form and top your pizza on a piece of parchment paper, tear all of the excess paper around the pizza and slide the peel underneath it to move the pizza into the oven that way. The paper will keep the dough from sticking to your peel. Make sure you really tear off any extra paper—it will turn to ash in the oven and blow into your pizza. The flash point for paper is 450°F (232°C), so you really don't want any extra paper in a 500°F (260°C) oven. And now you know why Ray Bradbury's book about book burning was called *Fahrenheit 451*. Promise me you'll practice with the peel, though; once you master it, after two or three pizzas you'll wonder how you ever had any trouble with it.

So maybe you only wanted one pizza and have extra dough. Oh, my friend. No. You have other things, too!

Monkey Bread

The perfect dessert to follow pizza or breakfast bread for the morning after a pizza party. The lower temp and longer cook time result in a squishier, more doughnut-like texture.

MAKES: 1 loaf

½ recipe Pizza Dough (page 45)

½ cup (115 g) butter

1 cup (192 g) sugar

2 tsp (5 g) ground cinnamon

Cut your pizza dough into 20 equal-size pieces and roll each piece into a ball shape. Grease a loaf pan.

Melt the butter. In a bowl, combine the sugar and cinnamon. This gets messy, so lay down a sheet of parchment paper under your work area to make cleanup a snap. Submerge the balls in the butter and then roll in the cinnamon-sugar mixture and place in the greased loaf pan, letting them eventually stack up. Allow the balls to rise in the loaf pan for 20 minutes.

Preheat the oven to 350°F (176°C).

Bake the bread for about 20 minutes and you have super yummy pull-apart monkey bread. This recipe is easily scaled if you find yourself with a ¼ recipe of pizza dough left; just use a smaller baking vessel. Once I made a baby batch in a crème brûlée ramekin that turned out great.

Troubleshooting Doughs

Dough not rising? It could be your yeast. It's a living organism, so if it's dead your dough isn't going to go anywhere. You can easily test its viability by mixing it in water with a pinch of sugar or flour. If it's alive, within 5 minutes you'll start to see some bubbles or a froth at the surface. If not, toss it. If you're planning on freezing your yeast-risen dough before baking, remember to add an extra pinch or two of yeast to counteract the inevitable death of some yeast.

Garlic Knots

Still more dough? That's exciting! Garlic knots are the perfect accompaniment to a big healthy salad. These have loads of delicious garlic butter, so line your rimmed aluminum sheet with parchment paper. They are too wet to put directly on the stone.

MAKES: 10 knots

½ recipe Pizza Dough (page 45)

½ cup (115 g) butter

3 large cloves garlic, crushed

½ tsp salt

¼ cup (45 g) grated Parmesan cheese

2 tbsp (5 g) chopped parsley, for garnish

Pinch of finishing salt (I prefer Maldon)

Portion the dough into 10 equal-sized pieces and roll into *bâtards* (fancy French word for bread logs). Let the bâtards rest while you prep the butter.

In a pan, melt the butter with the crushed garlic cloves and ½ teaspoon of salt and let it simmer for 5 minutes. Remove from the heat.

Line a rimmed aluminum sheet pan with parchment paper. Roll the bâtards into snakes about 6 inches (15 cm) long and tie them once or twice into a knot. Dip the knots into the garlic-butter mixture and place on the sheet pan. Sprinkle liberally with Parmesan cheese and allow to rise for 30 minutes.

Preheat the oven to 400°F (205°C).

Bake the knots for about 10 minutes. Again, check them for doneness—they should be a nice golden brown all over. Sprinkle with chopped parsley and finishing salt. I like to do mine in my toaster oven because it's usually a genius thought to make these in the middle of the night and using the large oven would take too long to heat up and/or at 1 a.m. I don't feel like removing all the pans I store in the oven.

Chapter 3

Let Me See You Jump! Jump!

Sauté After a Long Day

Sometimes, you just need dinner on the table. If that doesn't involve delivery, then you're probably making something on the stovetop. It's fast and the options are limitless. Let's take a closer look at what you're cooking with.

Pan Handling: The Best Materials for the Job

When you're ready to purchase a sauté pan, you definitely want to head to a store to get the feel of them. I like online shopping as much as the next person, but when it comes to equipment you'll be potentially using every day, do your diligence and see what feels best for you. Imagine it's full of food when you pick it up—they can be super heavy.

Stainless Steel

We talked a bit about stainless steel in our sheet pan chapter, but now we're using it for direct heat on the stovetop.

RECOMMENDED OR NOT: Yes, provided it's at minimum three layers thick.

PROS: The most common quality pans are at least three layers of metal bonded together. They have an inside and an outside of stainless steel and an inner core of either aluminum or copper, both excellent heat conductors. The combination of metals makes for good heat conduction and longevity of the product. Avoid anything that has a disk bottom. That just means the aluminum or copper is only on the bottom.

CONS: Truth is, stainless steel isn't the best heat conductor. A super-cheap sauté pan made from just stainless steel will heat your food unevenly, burning it in some areas, leaving it raw elsewhere and stuck on everywhere else, and it will likely warp. You want to get a bonded pan.

TO BUY: All-Clad D5 Brushed Stainless-Steel Skillet 10-inch (25-cm) for around $175. It's pricey, but it will last you forever.

The All-Clad has sealed edges; this will keep the layers from being exposed along the lip and becoming sharp or separating. Some higher end pans like Demeyere can have up to seven layers. These guys heat up fast; the price you pay is that they are *heavy* and the literal price you have to pay—oof, are they expensive (usually around $200 for a 9½ inch [24 cm]). I have one and have to admit that I love it. The extra layers make a difference and if it's "arm day" at the gym I can skip it.

Black/Carbon Steel

RECOMMENDED OR NOT: Yes.

PROS: I'm not sure why these haven't caught on in the United States yet. Most European homes have them and you've definitely eaten food made on one, because they are the standard in restaurants. They are relatively cheap, very sturdy and incredibly long lasting. I still find them to be pretty heavy and they just aren't as pretty hanging from a pot rack, but they are serious pans and deserve some respect. They typically run from $40 to $80 (more for artisanal pans made by hipsters).

CONS: What's tricky about them is that they turn a very dark brown or black, so it can be hard to gauge the amount of fond ("fond" is the delicious stuck-on food bits you develop while cooking and then later deglaze with a liquid. I am fond of fond) you've developed on the bottom, and if you don't dry them immediately after cleaning, they can rust. And I mean bone dry: the smallest amount of water will result in rust. Not a deal breaker, just something to know.

Cooking something acidic for a short period of time is okay, but a long, slow tomato sauce cook will strip the seasoning off and you'll have to reseason. FOLLOW THE PAN'S SEASONING INSTRUCTIONS! Anyone who complains about these pans likely didn't season it correctly. The pans are usually delivered coated in wax. Again, follow the instructions on how to season the pan. Likely you'll need to heat it in an oven over some towels to get most of the wax off and then have to get the rest with elbow grease.

Seasoning means the polymerization of oil on the surface through heat. The oil heats up and it fills in any microscopic nooks and crannies so that the surface is just as nonstick as an actual nonstick pan. It's magic, and the more you use it the better it gets! And since it's carbon steel, you can use it on an induction burner, gas, electric, in the oven or even on an open flame. The handles do get hot, but you can use a kitchen towel to keep your hand safe, or buy a silicone sleeve to go over the handle. Staub has recently released some beautiful cast-iron pans with a gorgeous and heat-resistant beechwood handle and I'm hoping they do the same for a carbon steel pan as well, hint hint. That might not work in the oven or on a campfire but it would be pretty great everywhere else.

Nonstick

RECOMMENDED OR NOT: YES. Well, some brands.

PROS: Everyone loves a nonstick pan; you don't have to use as much oil or butter and some of them will actually give you a really great sear and develop fond (I'm winking at you, Scanpan). They are lighter than five- or seven-ply stainless steel and you can get a decent variety that don't have PFOAs or Teflon in them, which are generally regarded nowadays to be potentially dangerous and have some definite heat limits.

CONS: If you get them too hot, the oil will polymerize. While it gives the carbon steel and cast iron a great nonstick coating, it will solidify on a nonstick pan, giving it an icky appearance. It just won't look clean anymore. Not all nonstick pans will work with an induction burner, so be sure you check that out first. You can be sure by bringing a refrigerator magnet with you when you're shopping. It should have a good strong hold with the pan.

Another thing to worry about with most nonstick pans is the coating coming off; "No, no, Carol, that must be um . . . pepper." It's gross and there's just no way it's good for you.

The Winner!

Over any other pan, I would buy the Scanpan. It's just a dream to work with. If I'm cooking with a higher heat (super high), I go with a carbon steel pan. Both of them are 12 inches (30 cm), so you have at least 9 inches (23 cm) of cooking surface. The Scanpan comes in a variety of price ranges and they are honestly all good. The handles are Bakelite, so you can put it in the oven. Since the nonstick properties are a part of the actual pan and not a coating, you don't have to worry about scratches or flecks of it coming off into your food, so go ahead and use a metal spatula. When I'm buying a pan as a gift, which is something I have done on more than one occasion, I get a Scanpan. A carbon steel pan requires a bit more work on the owner's behalf and a Scanpan is just easier. It's a matter of personal preference. I think they both outperform (the still-awesome) All-Clad tri-ply stainless steel skillet.

You may have noticed I didn't bring up copper. Copper is beautiful. It calls to us with its lustrous siren's song and shimmery color. Like all beautiful things, it can be a pain in the rear. It takes a lot of work to keep it looking good. It's not just beautiful, though. The most patina-ed copper pot is still a whiz at heat conduction. It's like driving a stick shift when you're used to an automatic. You can heat that baby up FAST and then cool it down fast, and back and forth. This much control takes a while to master, but when you do it's awesome. What's not awesome? How much it costs or the fact that cooking in copper can be dicey when there's something acidic involved like tomatoes or citrus. Most copper nowadays is lined with stainless steel, so you don't have to worry about that. Older pieces may be lined with tin, which will start to melt at around 450°F (232°C). You can have them re-tinned pretty cheaply, but I just find copper to be too expensive and fussy. Buy it for ornamental reasons or as a gift to your favorite author, but not for everyday cooking. Are you thinking of opening a caramel shop? A fruit jammery? Copper would probably make sense then.

The Stovetop–Sauté Pan Matrix

Now let's take a look at what type of stovetop that pan is going on. Let's break down the most popular range types.

ELECTRIC is cheaper to buy but more expensive to run—that's why you'll find them in a lot of rental units where the tenant is responsible for the utility bill. They can get hotter and work at lower temperatures than gas. The bottom drawers on electric ovens can be used as storage or some are made into warming drawers. They rely on electricity, which, depending on who your provider is, may or may not be fossil fuels. The tops tend to be glass, which is easier to clean than the original coils that used to be popular. Things like sugar are likely to stain the surface or be very difficult to remove.

GAS RANGES are slightly more expensive to buy and can be super expensive if you need to install a gas line but they are less expensive to operate. Still, this uses natural gas, something a lot of people are opposed to. Gas flames are easier to regulate—you see the flame. You know a big flame means high heat but a tiny flame can only get so tiny before it goes out and it's only heating up a specific spot in the pan. It works without electricity, though, if you're in an area prone to outages. You will either have a manual or an electric pilot light. If there's a flame that simply doesn't go out, then you have a pilot light. If you hear a clicking noise when you turn on the gas, then you have an electric starter with a regulator. These can get clogged fairly easily if you're a messy cook (no judgments). If you're having a hard time starting up the stovetop and still hear the clicking, that's a great place to start cleaning. Don't be afraid to dismantle it (some need to be unscrewed; put the screws in a jar as you go) and soak the regulator in some vinegar and warm soapy water for a moment. Give it a quick brush with an old toothbrush and poke around with a toothpick or cotton swab to clean it out. There's a small pinhole on the side where it usually lights from; send a needle through there. Dry and reassemble. If it's still not lighting, wait a few minutes and try again—it was likely just still wet.

INDUCTION is the most expensive to buy and the cheapest to run. In countries where it's super expensive to run electronics and gas prices are off the charts—like all of Scandinavia—induction has taken the lion's share of the marketplace. It's still run by electricity but has a significantly lower electrical draw from the outlet. It heats up the pan with magnets, so only the pan gets heated, not the surrounding air or area, thusly it can heat up significantly faster. You can boil water in 3 to 4 minutes, as opposed to 8 minutes and up. It also has the capacity to heat something at a much lower temp. It can operate as low as 101°F (38°C), which means you can do things directly in the pan that you would normally need a double boiler for, like melt chocolate or make fruit curds. The technology is getting cheaper. Some companies are working on hybrids—one or two induction burners next to a few gas burners—which is intriguing. I predict that by 2040, our personal robots will all be cooking on induction as we control them from our virtual cooking anti-gravity chambers in the other room.

CONS OF INDUCTION: Well, for a long time there was no glow. We need to see a light turn on to know if it's working, we can't just take a knob's word for it, so manufacturers have been adding a superfluous light to come on under our pans so we know it's working. I was using a portable induction burner on a *Food Network Challenge* once and was so nervous that it wasn't working that I kept sticking my finger on it to see if it was heating up. Oh sweetie, no, it won't heat up your finger when it's on. It only heats up pots. Duh.

The big catch is that you'll need induction-capable cookware. A magnet should stick to the pan strongly. Not all stainless steel is magnetic. If it has loads of chromium or aluminum added to it, it will be nice and shiny but not super magnetic. Feel free to bring a refrigerator magnet with you when you're perusing pots to be sure. You may also find that your digital thermometer doesn't work with induction. The magnetic field will screw with it, so you'll want to pull out your old analog thermometer and calibrate it before each use. Just stick it in a glass of ice water and it should read 32°F (0°C).

Other Tools of the Trade

FISH SPATULA: A flatter, wider spatula, this is great for picking up anything delicate from cookies to crepes.

OFFSET SPATULA: A small offset spatula is a tool in the coat pocket of most chefs. You can use it for everything from tasting food to nudging it to the side to make sure it releases, not to mention the frosting of cupcakes.

IMMERSION BLENDER: These are pretty cheap and super handy. With most models, you pop off the business end and hand wash it. They are small enough to store easily and a good option if you don't have room for a blender. I've had really good luck with the Cuisinart Smart Stick Immersion Blender, and at less than $30, it's a steal.

SILICONE SPATULA: One of the most reached-for tools, the silicone spatula can scrape down the sides of your mixing bowl or scoot around scrambled eggs with the greatest ease. They are heat resistant up to around 400°F (205°C) and the tops can pull off to be dish washed. They usually have wooden handles, which shouldn't make a trip through the dishwasher.

WIRE CAKE TESTER: These are just long wires with a little plastic handle. It's great for testing the doneness of fish without destroying it. Oh, and testing cakes and breads for doneness.

Tips for the Best Ingredients

Eggs

There's a lot of bologna out there in the egg market. The pictures of rolling pastures and idyllic farms on egg cartons are more often than not giant piles of hooey. The sad truth is most chickens have it pretty rough. Being free-range or cage-free might only mean there's a teeny door on one side of the coop the chickens aren't aware of and they are living with other chickens right on top of them. Your best bet is to look for "pastured chickens." These ladies get ideal living conditions, resulting in healthier, less stressed chickens. Happy chickens lay more nutritious eggs. Do they taste better? J. Kenji López-Alt over at Serious Eats did a pretty thorough taste test and surprisingly, they don't actually taste different. Pretty surprising considering their diet includes so much more than random chicken feed. They can eat grass, worms and bugs. That natural diet does make for a healthier egg, though. A 2010 Penn State study found that pastured eggs have twice as much vitamin E and long-chain omega-3 fatty acids—something we usually only get from salmon and walnuts. So, spring for the box of fancy pasture-raised eggs. You're helping out someone practicing sustainable humane farming and ounce for ounce it's STILL a great price for such a perfect protein. Can't justify the price? Then don't. It's still a great protein.

Fish

When you're buying fish, there are a few key characteristics to look for:

SMELL — it should smell like the ocean

TOUCH — when you poke it, there shouldn't be a huge crater left behind

LOOK – the scales should be largely intact for a whole fish and the eyes should be clear. Fillets should be shiny and not matte. If there's any liquid in the package, it should be clear, not milky. Milky = rotten.

Buy fish the same day you plan on preparing it. Fun fact: Any seafood you buy at the grocery store has been flash frozen at some point. Fish are prone to parasites and this is how they are killed. Even sushi-grade fish has been flash frozen. If you're buying something that's commonly frozen, like shrimp, buy it frozen; it's likely fresher and the flesh isn't so delicate that the product will have suffered. I love having a big bag of frozen shrimp in my freezer to supplement dinners where my kid doth protest against the main protein.

Grocery stores that sell live fish have special permits to do so. Don't go buying live clams out of some rando's trunk.

Many fish tend to come in pieces that don't match very well. There's a super-thin side that cooks really fast and a fat side that takes twice as long. A great way to convince them to cook at the same pace is to score the fish halfway down the skinny side and fold it under. It should be closer to the width of the fat part and will cook at the same rate.

Those little bones can be tricky to remove but even worse to chomp down on. The easiest way to remove the offending bones is to lay the fillet over the back of an inverted bowl—the bones will magically present themselves for plucking. Use a dedicated set of flat-ended tweezers that you keep for just this purpose. Needle-nose pliers also work well. If the bones are staying hidden, draw your finger along the center 3 inches (7.6 cm) a few times to tease them out.

FARM VS. WILD: All salmon is good for you, right? Well, that's a little tricky. Salmon is one of the few sources of omega-3 fatty acids. Omega-3 keeps your blood healthy, joints lubricated, lowers depression and inflammation and promotes brain health! It's great and we should all probably be eating more of it. Both versions of salmon have omega-3s but the farmed version is much fattier—that's why it's lighter in color. Wild salmon is going to be a much darker pinky-orange. If it's pale, it's likely been farmed and all that extra fat makes it pale. With all that extra fat comes a lot of extra omega-6. The general consensus is that this isn't ideal but it's still worth buying farmed salmon to increase your omega-3 intake. If that was all we had to worry about it would be great. Unfortunately, a lot of salmon farms have some other nasty problems and contaminants that the fish can't exactly get away from. If you can swing it, buy line-caught wild salmon; if not, you might want to do more research and limit your farmed salmon dinners to just once or twice a month.

Root Vegetables

Carrots and potatoes have incredibly thin to almost nonexistent peels. They absorb everything through the soil. Pesticides don't just sit on their surface but are absorbed. When it comes to things grown in the dirt, you're really better off buying organic. Things with thick skins like melons, avocados, mangoes and coconut are some examples of food that you don't need to spring for the organic versions of.

The Best Techniques for Sautéing

"Sauté" literally means to jump up and land in the same position. To use this as a cooking technique is a great trick. Ironically, you don't use a sauté pan, you use a frying pan, one with slightly sloped edges that will enable you to make whatever you're cooking dance. It needs to slide up a ramp, not bang into a wall. What we call a "sauté pan" has completely vertical sides, no jumping allowed, but frying in them works like a charm. They also keep more of the steam in, so if you're trying to get a nice crust on something, the wrong pan might make it a bit mushy if you crowd it—you didn't spend all that money to get a rubbery steak!

To sauté something, you'll likely need some fat in the pan to reduce the friction, unless it's a brand-new nonstick pan. Grab the handle and lift the pan up 3 to 5 inches (7.6 to 13 cm). Tilt it forward and, moving your arm more than your wrist, quickly scoot the ingredients down to the far edge; then, lifting the front slightly, flip them back to the center of the pan. It takes a little practice. A great way to perfect the motion is to fill a pan with half a cup of dry rice and try it over a noncarpeted area until you get the hang of it.

Salmon with White Wine and Tarragon Sauce

This is my go-to salmon dish. It is both simple and elegant—something we should all strive for. I always have salmon fillets in my freezer for an easy dinner. When you're ready to prepare them, half an hour in tepid water will defrost them. After the salmon cooks, you'll be deglazing the pan with wine, so cleanup is a breeze and no tasty morsels are left behind. Your carbon steel or nonstick (non-Teflon) pan will work best here.

SERVES: 4

2 tbsp (30 ml) grapeseed oil or refined coconut oil

1½ lb (680 g) salmon fillet, skin on or off

4 tsp (21 g) Dijon mustard

1 shallot, minced

¼ cup (60 ml) white wine

2 tbsp (29 g) butter, cold

1 tsp chopped fresh tarragon

Juice of ½ lemon

Salt and pepper

Heat a swirl of grapeseed oil in your pan over medium-high heat. As it heats, it will become less viscous and coat the bottom of the pan. Pat dry your salmon fillets and coat with a thin layer of the mustard. Place the salmon fillets in the pan, being careful to let them drop away from you to avoid any splattering hot oil. Cook the salmon for 3 minutes, and then flip to finish the other side.

Check the fish for doneness by poking between the flakes with a cake tester. You can see if the fish is cooked through if it separates easily, and a cake tester won't leave as large a hole as a blade. Move the fish to a cutting board to rest. Add the chopped shallot to the pan and cook for 1 to 2 minutes to soften.

Add the wine to the pan and reduce to 1 to 2 tablespoons (15 to 30 ml). Add the cold butter and tarragon and stir around to be sure that all of the fond from the bottom of the pan is loosened. Finish the sauce with a squeeze from half a lemon, a pinch of salt and a crank of pepper.

Serving Method 1: Plate the salmon and pour the sauce on top.

Serving Method 2: Add 5 or 6 handfuls of fresh baby spinach to the sauce, turning with a set of tongs to wilt and cover the spinach. Pile up the wilted spinach in wine sauce on your plate and top with fish.

Crazy for Crepes

Crepes are the first thing I was ever taught how to make. I was nine years old and it meant a lot to me that a person in a place of authority would hand me a large knife and crepe pan without hesitation. This was amazing! These are confidence-boosting skills. You wake up at a slumber party and casually mention, "Oh, should I make us all crepes?" Boom! You're a badass! Get the youth in your life involved in the kitchen! You don't necessarily need a crepe pan; your non-Teflon nonstick pan will work great for this. I wouldn't even attempt it on a stainless steel pan.

MAKES: 8–10 crepes

2 large eggs

¾ cup (177 ml) milk

½ cup (120 ml) water

1 cup (100 g) flour

3 tbsp (43 g) melted butter, plus more for the pan

2 tsp (8 g) sugar and 1 tsp vanilla for sweeter crepes (optional)

Combine all of the ingredients in a blender and pulse for 10 seconds. The batter will keep for up to 48 hours if you would like to make it the night before.

Heat a small nonstick, well-seasoned black steel or crepe pan over medium heat. Add butter to coat and then wipe it out with a paper towel. Too much butter will burn the crepe and make it more difficult to maneuver, but a little bit will help it brown slightly.

Pour 1 ounce (30 ml) of batter into the center of the pan for small crepes, or 2 ounces (60 ml) for larger crepes, and swirl to spread evenly. You can fill a shot glass with crepe batter and pour that in if it's easier for you than pouring from the bowl, or use a small ladle. Cook until the batter goes from shiny to matte and no more bubbles are surfacing, about 30 seconds. Tug one side up and slide a fish spatula under and flip. If you're feeling adventurous, use a pair of tongs. Cook for another 10 seconds and remove to a cutting board. Lay them out flat so they can cool. Continue until all the batter is gone, feeling free to stack them on top of each other.

After they have cooled, you can stack them and store in sealable plastic bags in the refrigerator for several days or in the freezer for up to 2 months. Thaw your frozen crepes before pulling them apart.

Potential fillings include:

- Strawberry and Nutella
- Lox and cream cheese
- Ham and Gruyère

- Maple syrup
- Scrambled eggs
- Spinach and goat cheese

The options are limitless, so use your imagination and leftovers!

Tortilla Espanola ala Michelle

This is a classic Spanish tapas dish that is as delicious at room temperature as it is hot from the pan. I cheat by finishing it in the oven, which keeps it super simple to prepare and less greasy. This makes for a delicious and satisfying dinner with a little side salad and keeps for days in the fridge. I always use my Scanpan for this so that I can count on its nonstick nature and still pop it in the oven.

SERVES: 4 as a main or 8 as an appetizer

8 eggs

Salt and pepper

2 tbsp (30 ml) olive oil

3 large Yukon Gold potatoes, peeled and sliced into 1/8" (3-mm) rounds

1 large shallot, thinly sliced

1 clove garlic, minced

2 tsp (4 g) dried herbes de Provence

1 cup (150 g) chopped precooked chorizo, crumbled (optional)

6 oz (170 g) goat cheese (optional)

Preheat the oven to 400°F (205°C).

In a large bowl, lightly beat the eggs and season with a generous sprinkle of salt and pepper. Feel free to whip out that immersion blender if you have one. Set the egg mixture aside.

In a 12-inch (30-cm) ovenproof, nonstick skillet, heat the olive oil over medium-low heat until it is warm. The potatoes take the longest to cook, so add them first and sauté for 2 minutes. Add the sliced shallot and gently cook until translucent, about 5 minutes. Add the minced garlic and sprinkle in the herbes de Provence and crumbled chorizo (if using). Cook the entire mixture over medium-low heat for another 10 minutes to marry the flavors and release the oils in the dried herbes de Provence mixture. If anything starts to get color, lower the heat.

Give the pan a shimmy to evenly distribute the ingredients. Pour over the eggs gently and shimmy again. Allow the mixture to cook on the stovetop until the edges begin to set and the center starts to look thicker. Dollop the goat cheese on top (if using) and move the skillet to the oven. If you're worried about accidentally grabbing the handle, wrap it loosely with foil to give you a little alert not to touch.

Bake for 5 minutes or until the center is no longer jiggly. Upon removal from the oven, tug back the edges or slide your small offset spatula in between the edges and the pan to make sure they aren't stuck to the sides. If there's resistance, you can add some butter to melt down the sides and help it to release.

Invert a plate or wooden cutting board on the pan and flip it to release the tortilla. The tortilla should be nice and golden on the outside while remaining creamy and gooey on the inside. Serve hot or at room temperature.

Quick Happy Chicken

Sometimes you just need to get dinner on the table fast. This quick recipe is so simple and delicious, I make it even when I have all the time in the world. The sauce is luscious with fun pops of saltiness from the capers. I like to use a stainless steel pan for this so I can really see everything in the pan as it cooks. Browned butter is harder to see in a dark nonstick pan.

SERVES: 2 for dinner or 4 for a lighter lunch

2 boneless, skinless chicken breasts, filleted to make 4 thin pieces

½ cup (50 g) all-purpose flour

1 tsp salt

1 tsp pepper

1 tbsp (15 ml) refined oil

4 tbsp (57 g) unsalted butter

1 shallot, chopped

2 tsp (6 g) capers

1 tbsp (2.5 g) minced sage

1 anchovy, minced

Juice of ½ lemon

Place the thin pieces of chicken between sheets of plastic wrap and bang the heck out of them with a rolling pin or rubber mallet until they are approximately ¼ inch (6 mm) thick. By thinning the chicken, we reduce our cooking time by two-thirds.

Place your flour, salt and pepper onto a large plate and swirl with your finger to mix. Lightly dredge the chicken pieces through the flour mixture and place on a paper towel off to the side. You only need a thin coating, which will help the chicken brown. Any flour that is left in the pan will help thicken the pan sauce.

Heat your pan over medium-high heat and add a refined oil of your choice. Extra virgin olive oil and other unrefined oils have more polyphenols floating around in them—yummy raw but they fill your house up with smoke and smell like fuel when they overheat. Swirl the oil around until it starts to shimmer and gently lay in 2 of your cutlets. Don't crowd the pan and try to cook them all at once. They will take about 4 minutes per side. Flip with tongs when they are golden brown. Repeat until all the chicken is cooked, tenting finished pieces with foil as you complete them.

Add the butter (or fat of your choice) to the pan. As it bubbles up, add in your shallot to soften for about 2 minutes. Add in the capers, sage and minced anchovy, which will dissolve, so you don't have to tell anyone that's why it tastes so good. When the sauce is reduced down and you have scraped up any extra fond, finish it with a squirt of lemon juice and serve with rice or some fluffy, quick quinoa.

Jumping Carrots

Carrots are hard. Physically, not in a "grew up on the streets and been to prison" kind of way. Quick cooking isn't really something we associate with carrots, but with this blanching hack, you can serve up any hard veggie in a minimum amount of time and very little effort. Reach for the pan that you feel most comfortable sautéing with. It should be light enough to manipulate with a carrot party going on inside.

SERVES: 4 as a side

1 lb (450 g) baby carrots

¼ cup (60 ml) water

3 tbsp (43 g) unsalted butter

2 tbsp (28 g) brown sugar

Salt and pepper

Pumpkin pie spice or ground cinnamon (optional)

Spread your carrots around the bottom of your pan, making sure that there is enough room for them all to have contact with the bottom of the pan. Add the water and turn your heat on to medium-high. Cover the top with a lid or foil and let the water come to a boil for about 4 minutes. Remove the foil and let the rest of the water boil off.

When the pan is dry, add the butter, sugar and seasonings. If you're feeling particularly autumnal, go ahead and add some pumpkin pie spice or cinnamon. Toss the carrots around or move around manually with a spatula until the carrots begin to brown and blister. Plate, adding any juices left in the pan.

Better Than Take-Out Teriyaki Chicken

I love eating take-out as much as the next person, but making these go-to staples that everyone loves means I can keep an eye on the amount of sugar and sodium that go in—two things that restaurants tend to be a little heavy-handed with. A quick sauté is all we need to bring this satisfying dinner together!

SERVES: 4

SAUCE

¼ cup (60 ml) honey

2 tbsp (30 ml) apple cider vinegar

¼ cup (60 ml) low-sodium soy sauce

1 tsp grated ginger

2 cloves garlic, grated or minced

1 tbsp (9 g) cornstarch

CHICKEN

1–2 tbsp (15–30 ml) grapeseed or peanut oil

1½ lb (680 g) cubed chicken breast

Salt and pepper

1 tbsp (10 g) sesame seeds

½ cup (25 g) sliced green onions

To make the sauce, in a small bowl, whisk together the honey, vinegar, soy sauce, ginger, garlic and cornstarch and set aside.

To make the chicken, heat your sauté pan or wok over medium-high heat and swirl in 1 to 2 tablespoons (15 to 30 ml) of oil to coat.

Season the cubed chicken with salt and pepper, and add to the pan. Cook while frequently stirring to ensure even cooking, 3 to 4 minutes.

Add the sauce to the chicken and continue to cook, bringing the sauce up to a boil so that it thickens and coats the chicken. Break apart a few pieces of chicken to ensure it's cooked throughout.

Serve over rice with steamed broccoli and garnish with sesame seeds and green onion.

Chapter 4

Heavy Metal

It's (Cast) Iron, Man

It's a pretty good bet that if you buy a cast-iron pan, you'll have it for life and hopefully pass it along after that. A good cast-iron piece should long outlive you and if you're trying to pare down the number of tools in your kitchen, then you can't do much better than the multipurpose cast-iron skillet.

The Best Tools for the Job

Most cast-iron pans come preseasoned now, making it even easier. I don't mean they're salted. Seasoning in this context means that they have been made naturally nonstick with a coating of oil and then heated up. Remember how we talked about not overheating oils or they would polymerize? Well, we want that here. That natural polymer coating is what fills in all the microscopic nooks and crannies, making our skillet nonstick. What's also amazing? They're usually pretty cheap! I have tried a ton of them (and they can weigh a ton) and my favorite is a tie between the pan from Victoria (made in Canada) and Lodge (made in the United States). The Victoria pan has a slightly longer handle and a larger helper handle, making it easier to pick up (did I mention they are heavy?). They are both in the mid-$20 range, so either one is a steal in my book; I actually own one of each. Another brand to check out is the Field Company cast-iron pan. This family set out to create a smoother and lighter pan, making it even more nonstick and easy to move. They'll run you about $100, which is worth it if you're concerned about the weight.

What about enameled cast iron? If you've ever set foot in a Sur La Table or Williams Sonoma, surely your eyes were drawn to the shelves of glittering Staub and Le Creuset. Even the most serious chef will stop for a moment and dreamily whisper, "preeeeeeetty." These are serious pieces, though, with some serious price tags. So, what's the difference? The pieces are all made out of heavyweight cast iron, just like our Lodge and Victoria pans, but these are enameled on the outside AND inside. They are resistant to rust, chipping and cracking and don't require any additional seasoning. You're not going to have to reseason after a slow cook pan lasagna with these guys. The only drawback is that they aren't quite as indestructible. Eventually the enamel can chip. If the chip is on the outside,

it's still usable! Just not aesthetically pleasing. Lodge has also gotten into the enamel cast-iron game at a lower price point and they are just as good. They heat up the same way as naked cast iron but you can slow cook tomato-heavy stews in them without stripping them. I save my enameled cast-iron purchases for Dutch ovens and go with regular cast iron for sauté pans.

Find a beautiful piece of cast iron at a garage sale but it's rusty and gross? You can totally save it. Scrub off that rust with some steel wool and then you can season the pan. Once it's clean and dry, apply a thin coat of a flaxseed oil or lard to your pan and place it on a cookie sheet in a low oven for about 40 minutes. It may need to be done more than once to get it as slick as a nonstick pan, but it will get there.

PROS: Iron is not a super-even heat conductor. What it does do is heat the heck up and retain that heat, giving you a beautiful sear. It's relatively easy to reseason a pan to keep it naturally nonstick without the use of chemicals or Teflon coating. Pans are cheap and, with proper care, will last a lifetime. Cast iron can go from stovetop to oven easily.

CONS: Heavy. Super heavy. It's definitely not for an active arm flip sauté, but it's great for everything else. The handles get hot whether you're cooking on the stovetop or in an oven. By no means is this dishwasher safe! Pans must be gently hand cleaned and dried immediately to avoid rusting.

Other Tools of the Trade

MELON BALLER: I use my melon baller at least five times a week and almost never to make balls out of melons. It's the absolute best at taking the seeds and stems out of apples and pears. It's how you get swoon-worthy poached pears (that we cover in the Dutch oven chapter). I also use the melon baller to fish out cocktail onions, maraschino cherries and capers. It's the world's tiniest sieve.

KITCHEN SHEARS: I'm talking dedicated kitchen shears, not sometimes crafting scissors that end up under a bunch of papers on the desk. These are stronger than regular scissors, able to cut through bone! Some of them even come apart for easier cleaning. If you're cutting through a lot of chickens, then go for the Wüsthof Poultry Shears. They curve up at the end to tuck right into a bird; they're super strong and the most expensive are around $80. For more all-purpose shears, I like the Wüsthof Come-Apart Kitchen Shears for around $20.

THERMOMETER: A digital thermometer is a must-have. They register super fast; just be sure to only submerge them about halfway through the meat, as touching the bottom of the pan or a bone can give you a false reading. Wash only the probe section and then sanitize it with some vinegar after you're done.

SPLATTER GUARD: An absolute must if you ever fry anything! This fine metal mesh circle with a long handle can be rested on top of your pan to keep drops of hot oil from making a mess, or worse, burning you. They'll get discolored from the exposure to high heat, which is totally fine. Just be cautious of the metal handle getting hot if you leave it on a pan for more than a few minutes. You can pick one up for around $10.

Tips for the Best Ingredients

Oats

The main difference between steel-cut (aka Irish oats) and rolled oats is how they are processed. Both are whole grains, but rolled oats are steamed, rolled and then steamed again, resulting in flat flakes. Steel-cut oats are just chopped up oat kernels. Because of this, steel-cut oats take longer to digest, leaving you feeling full longer, and they are lower on the glycemic index (no sugar spikes). Mixing the two gives you the best of both worlds. I find when I use 100 percent steel-cut oats in a recipe, my jaw gets tired from all the chewing. The rough texture of steel-cut oats makes them less than ideal for baking, so stick with the rolled oats for that.

Quick-cooking oats have been steamed and rolled even more than rolled oats. This extra processing results in an oat that cooks up super fast and super creamy but, alas, it's not all good. That extra processing makes it easier for us to digest it quickly, which means it's not nearly as filling and your sugar will spike much faster.

Canned Tomatoes

My absolute favorite cans of tomatoes come from Muir Glen. They have a wonderful balance of sweetness and acidity, they are organically grown in California and most importantly, they are packed in a vinyl-lined tin. Most tomatoes come in BPA-lined tins. The super-acidic tomatoes leach out the BPA and you end up eating it. Blech.

Olive Oil

Extra-virgin olive oil is a staple in our kitchen. It's delicious raw or cooked and it's high in monounsaturated fatty acids (healthy fats). When you're buying olive oil, don't go for the gallon jug at the big box store unless you're seriously going to go through it within six months. Oil will go rancid and the flavors degrade pretty quickly, so just buy what you'll use in a month or two tops.

Olive oil has a lower smoke point (410°F [210°C]) than canola or peanut oil, but you can feel free to cook with it in a lot of lower heat applications. When you heat up a fancy olive oil, you kill off the polyphenols, the compounds that make it yummy, so don't reach for a super-fancy bottle to roast veggies with—save that for dipping or salad dressings.

Olive oil has been in the news a lot recently as a commonly mislabeled product. There's actually a police team in Italy dedicated to the eradication of olive oil fraud. I've been very happy with the California Olive Ranch's extra-virgin olive oil. Whatever you buy, it should be in a dark glass bottle and ideally have a harvest date listed. You'll want to buy oil that's less than a year old, if possible.

Pork Chops

Pork chops have a bad habit of impersonating hockey pucks. For decades we've been overcooking them, terrified that they might have parasites. The odds of getting trichinosis from eating pork sold at retail stores is only 1 in 154 million. So, by all means, just cook these babies to 145°F (63°C).

The most foolproof cut to choose is a blade-end chop. It has the closest thing to a marbling of fat with several ribbons tracing through it. Rib and center-cut chops are all pretty to look at but they tend to have dense areas of meat with no fat; you'll definitely want to make sure you're serving a sauce with them. Go for chops that are about 1 inch (2.5 cm) thick with the bone in.

Since pork is relatively lean and the fat tends to dart through it in ribbons as opposed to marbling, they tend to curl up, losing precious cooking surface area. The fat and meat cook at different rates, so when the fat shrinks it pulls everything else up with it. There are two ways around this. You can score the fat along the outside every inch (2.5 cm) or so or you can start in a cold pan and let the pan and chop slowly heat up together.

Avoid "enhanced" pork chops. They have lip injections and hair plugs. Just kidding. What they do have is a salty liquid injected into them. I'm all for brining your pork, but this sits in the meat way too long, resulting in a spongy pork chop.

The Best Techniques for Cooking with Cast Iron

Cast iron is easiest to clean when it's still hot. You can plunge it into hot water (never cold or it could crack or warp) and a few passes with a sponge should do the trick. There's also a type of chain mail on the market (it looks like a medieval washcloth) that is great at cleaning out food and leaving the seasoning behind. Amagabeli makes a good one that runs about $13. They are fun to play with, so good luck keeping it away from your kids if you have them. You may have heard to never use soap on them. If your seasoning is truly built up, then soap shouldn't be a problem. Know that every time

you cook you're building up that layer of seasoning, so if a small spot starts to look grayish instead of black, just avoid making tomato sauces in it for a few days and it should self-correct. Speaking of tomato sauces, highly acidic food can break down the polymers you formed and require you to reseason the pan. I'm talking long time in the oven baked tomato sauce dishes. Cooking something with tomato sauce quickly shouldn't have any adverse effects on your pan.

Cast iron is best for heating up super hot and retaining that heat as well as developing a natural nonstick surface. This consistency of heat is great for frying things and getting a great sear because it's very effective at keeping the temperature stable. It's also super great at going from the stovetop to the oven, so baking breads in it is a no-brainer.

Be careful not to overheat your cast iron without at least a coating of oil; the seasoning layer can be burned off if it's heated up naked! Be liberal with your fats! Cast iron is very strong and very heavy but also surprisingly very brittle. Be careful not to drop it or the likelihood of it breaking in half is very high. If you're only going to get one cast-iron pan, make it as big as you can comfortably carry. Imagine it's full when you test it out.

Cut with a Knife

RECOMMENDED OR NOT: Yes! You should always cut things with a knife, never teeth. What were you thinking?!?

Seriously, though, knives are one of the most important if not the MOST important tool a cook can wield, not to mention a potentially very serious investment. Your knife is a very personal tool. This is your knife. There are many, many knives, but this one is yours, so show it some respect.

Chef's knives (long curved blades as opposed to the flat edge of a Santoku) come in both German and Japanese styles, with the main difference being the angle that the business end is ground to. Put simply, the German blades are slightly heavier and thicker and are cut at a wider angle, which means they are sharp and can hold their edge for a long time. Japanese blades are ground to a finer edge, which means they are super sharp and physically lighter. This can mean more maintenance (but a finer cut). They come in 6-, 8- and 10-inch (15-, 20- and 25-cm) lengths. The 6-inch (15-cm) is okay if you're just starting out and are intimidated by the larger knives, and the 10-inch (25-cm) is good if you're already comfortable with knives and have the need for something with that much edge. I find that most chefs consistently reach for the 8-inch (20-cm) blade. It's perfect for almost every cutting task. The curved edge lets you rock the knife back and forth for quick chopping. Go to the store and try them out. Imagine you have olive oil on your hands: Is it slippery? Bring an apple with you. Hey, you're probably about to drop over $100, so they will let you chop your apple.

Store your knives on a magnetic strip on the wall if possible. This will keep the edge from dulling by sliding into a wooden block or getting dinged in the drawer. If you insist on a wooden storage block, then opt for the kind that store the knives sideways to avoid dulling the edges.

Clean your knives in warm soapy water, never the dishwasher even though some brands are technically dishwasher safe. The high heat and chemicals will actually weaken the steel and dull the edge.

CARE: The long pointy steel rod that comes with most knife kits isn't for poking people away from your food. It's used to hone the edge of your knife. Hone! Not sharpen. It doesn't take any steel off of your blade but realigns the microscopic edge. With use, the sharp edge of the knife will eventually roll to one side, making it feel dull. Honing it regularly (I do it three to five times a week) will keep it feeling sharp. Simply hold the knife about a matchbook's distance from the steel and slide down in an arcing motion from the base to the tip. Five to ten times on each side should do it. Apply a safe amount of pressure as you do this—you're moving steel.

Have your blades professionally sharpened once a year or take a knife skills class to learn how to do it yourself. Knives are expensive and sharpening isn't something you should try to wing on your own.

What to Buy

Again, this depends on personal preference and cooking habits. I recommend that you start with three knives: a paring knife for small jobs; a serrated blade for tomatoes, cakes and bread; and a chef's knife for everything else. Don't buy the big old knife set. You should test each one and build your own collection.

Best Budget Option

VICTORINOX 8-INCH (20-CM), $35–$45: This is a great entry into the field. The handle is a bulky black plastic and it holds an edge for a nice long time. This is a stamped steel knife, which is cheaper to manufacture, hence the smaller price tag.

ZWILLING J.A. HENCKELS INTERNATIONAL 8-INCH (20-CM) CLASSIC, $50: The steel extending the full length of the knife means good balance. This baby is a workhorse.

Best Upgrade Options

GLOBAL 7-INCH HOLLOW-EDGE ASIAN CHEF'S KNIFE, $80: The entire knife is one piece of steel, and yes, it's only 7 inches (17.8 cm), which makes it pretty nimble. The dimples on the edge help to prevent food from sticking to it. Their classic dimple-less knife is around $130.

ZWILLING J. A. HENCKELS PRO TRADITIONAL CHEF'S KNIFE, $140: Another workhorse, this knife has a really comfortable bolster, which is great at preventing hand fatigue if you need to chop a million onions.

Best Fancy Options

SHUN 9-INCH (23-CM) CLASSIC WESTERN, $165: Shun makes my favorite Japanese knives. This is what I reach for when I'm chopping veggies or fish. It has a core of extra-strong "super steel" and the handle feels really great in my tiny hands. The Shun Hiro knife comes in around $300, but it's gorgeous and more durable. It's a piece of art, though, and you'll want to hang it on the wall.

WÜSTHOF CLASSIC WIDE 8-INCH (20-CM), $175: I love this knife. It has a nice wide blade and the heft of it helps to power through big projects like pineapples or butternut squash.

Heart-Warming Apple Baked Oatmeal

Cast iron can go seamlessly from the stovetop to the oven with this perfect, all-season, hearty breakfast that's as good hot from the pan as it is cold from the fridge. This will fill you up! And it's also heart-healthy, so you'll get to feel all smug. What could be better? I like to use both steel-cut and rolled oats to give it some extra textural interest, but feel free to just use one variety if that's all you have on hand.

SERVES: 6 generously, or 12 as part of a larger brunch spread

1 cup (161 g) steel-cut oats

1 cup (80 g) rolled oats

1 tsp baking powder

1 tsp cardamom

1½ tsp (4 g) ground cinnamon

1 tsp ground ginger

¼ cup (33 g) pumpkin seeds

½ cup (58 g) chopped walnut pieces

1 tbsp (10 g) flax seeds

¼ tsp salt

2–3 apples, cut into ½" (13-mm) cubes

2 tsp (10 ml) pure vanilla extract

3½ cups (828 ml) boiling water

¼ cup (60 ml) maple syrup or honey (optional)

Preheat the oven to 375°F (190°C) and bring a pot of water to a boil.

Heat your cast-iron skillet over medium heat, then add the oats and stir to toast for 2 to 3 minutes.

Add the baking powder, spices, pumpkin seeds and walnut pieces and continue to toast for 1 more minute; this heats up the oils and intensifies their flavors. Add the flax and salt, and stir to mix. Add the apples and vanilla, and pour the boiling water over the mixture; pat it down to evenly hydrate. Drizzle with syrup or honey if using.

Bake for 40 minutes. If you would like a slightly darker apple, broil for the last 3 minutes.

Alternatively, you could use pears or bananas, or add in some chocolate chips or dried fruit. The options are limitless.

Zucchini Fries with Aioli

Deep frying a healthy vegetable is a fun party trick. Smaller items are easy to fry off in a cast-iron pan. Because the pan has great heat retention, you can run through multiple batches. Keep an eye on that oil temp, though! With a cast-iron pan, you can lower your heat to medium as soon as it hits 375°F (190°C) and it will likely keep the heat close to that for as long as you need to fry off these babies.

SERVES: 6

ZUCCHINI FRIES

Canola oil, for deep frying

3 zucchinis, ends trimmed and cut into ½" (13-mm) strips

Salt

2 eggs, beaten

½ cup (60 g) panko bread crumbs

¼ cup (45 g) Parmesan cheese

AIOLI

2 cloves garlic, minced

Salt

1 egg yolk

2 tsp (10 ml) lemon juice

½ tsp Dijon mustard

¼ cup (60 ml) extra-virgin olive oil

3 tbsp (45 ml) canola oil

To make the zucchini fries, heat 1½ inches (4 cm) of canola oil in a deep pot to 375°F (190°C).

Place the sliced zucchini on a paper towel to dry and sprinkle lightly with salt.

In a bowl, whisk the two eggs with a pinch of salt until it is liquefied. On a plate, swirl the panko crumbs with the Parmesan. Set up your dredging station so that step one is dipping the zucchini in the egg mixture, then coating it with the bread crumb mixture and then into the oil.

Gently lower the zucchini into the oil. Cook for 3 to 5 minutes, until caramel brown. Remove with a spider to paper towels to drain.

To make the aioli, using the back of a spoon, mash the minced garlic with a pinch of salt in a medium bowl. Whisk the garlic together with the egg yolk, lemon juice and mustard. In a separate bowl, add both of the oils together and then slooooowly stream them into the mixture, whisking until a thick mayonnaise consistency is reached. If it's a little too thick, whisk in a few drops of water. If you're having trouble with the bowl moving around, place a wet towel under the bowl to keep it in place.

Troubleshooting Frying

It's a bummer when all of a sudden, you realize your oil has started to smoke. Hot oil is NO JOKE. And once it's hot, it takes forever to cool down. You can add ½ to 1 cup (120 to 240 ml) of room-temperature oil carefully to bring the temperature back down to working range. If you fry in oil that's too hot, the food will look gorgeous and cook fast. Problem is, the inside will be totally raw. On the other hand, if it's too cold, then the food is likely to go mushy from hanging out in the oil too long. Don't just dump your oil! As long as it's not fishy, you can put the oil back into its original vessel. Just use a funnel lined with a few coffee filters. It will be slightly darker in color but totally fine to use again.

Faye-berts

Remember the magical heat-retention properties of cast iron? In this recipe, we heat up the pan first and then add the batter. The explosion of heat gives us a showstopping poof of a pancake known as a Dutch baby. Don't just relegate this recipe to breakfast—this is an awesome dessert too. It only takes maybe five minutes to put it together. That's some serious return on investment! My best friend Rachel married a lovely Dutch guy and moved to Amsterdam to make her own Dutch baby, Faye. Please don't squirt the real Faye with lemon wedges.

SERVES: 4

3 eggs

½ cup (50 g) all-purpose flour

½ cup (120 ml) milk

1 tsp vanilla extract

1 tbsp (12 g) sugar

Pinch of ground nutmeg or cinnamon

4 tbsp (57 g) butter

Preheat the oven to 450°F (232°C).

Combine everything but the butter in a large bowl and whisk, or even easier, combine it in your blender and give it a whirl, or pull out your immersion blender to make even quicker work of it.

Add the butter in your 10-inch (25-cm) cast-iron pan and let it melt in the oven. Once it's melted (about 3 minutes), open the door and pour all the batter into the pan and shut the oven door. Bake for 20 to 25 minutes or until the pancake poofs up and turns golden brown.

Serve warm with a sprinkling of powdered sugar and lemon wedges for squeezing. Whipped cream and berries are always an option too!

Juicy Lip-Smacking Pork Chops

Cast iron gives us the perfect surface to get a nice, crusty sear on our chops. The pan does double duty by cooking our apples to perfection when the pork chops are finished. They're the perfect time occupier to make sure you let the meat rest!

SERVES: 4

PORK CHOPS

4 bone-in pork chops, about 1" (2.5 cm) thick

Salt and pepper

1 tbsp (15 ml) canola oil

1 tbsp (14 g) unsalted butter

TOPPING APPLES

2 tbsp (30 g) unsalted butter

½ cup (110 g) packed brown sugar

¼ tsp ground cinnamon

¼ tsp ground cloves

1 Granny Smith apple, peeled and sliced or cubed

½ cup (120 ml) apple cider

Salt and pepper

To make the pork chops, pat dry the pork chops and season both sides with salt and pepper. You can do this step 1 day in advance to tenderize the meat further.

Heat the oil in a large cast-iron skillet over medium-high heat. Add the chops and cook, turning them over every other minute to evenly caramelize both sides. Add the butter to the pan and turn off the heat; cast iron is great at retaining heat and will continue to effectively cook your chops. Continue to flip the chops to coat with butter.

Insert an instant read thermometer into the thickest part of a chop and remove when it reaches 140°F (60°C). The chop will continue to cook as it rests on the cutting board, reaching up to 145°F (63°C).

To make the topping apples, add the butter, brown sugar, cinnamon, cloves and apples to the pan; no need to clean the pan if you're serving these with the pork chops. Cook the apples over medium heat, stirring occasionally, until the apples are nicely caramelized and softened. Add the apple cider and reduce it until the sauce is thick and syrupy. Be gentle with the apples now as they've become quite soft. Season with salt and pepper if it will be served with something savory; leave as is for an ice cream or oatmeal topping.

Take a Rest

When meat cooks, it constricts, like a muscle flexing. Think of it like a wet sponge inside a ziplock bag. If you squeeze the sponge, the water will be collected in the bag. If you immediately slice open the bag, a lot of that water is going to come rushing out. If you wait a few minutes, the sponge will reabsorb some of that water. It's the same principle with meat. The worst thing you can do is dig right into it after it comes out of the pan. It only takes 5 minutes to rest.

Vulcan Roasted Chicken

OK, it's not really Vulcan. It's a chicken that has been spatchcocked—a word I have a very hard time remembering and I tend to think of it as Spock-ed chicken, even though the right word sounds much more Klingon. Whole roasted chickens take a long time to cook, but a spatchcocked chicken cooks in a fraction of the time. This recipe with carrots and parsley is a real beauty. Feel free to swap out the carrots with fingerling potatoes.

SERVES: 4

One 3- to 4-lb (1.3–1.8-kg) whole chicken

Salt and pepper

1 tbsp (15 ml) refined olive oil (unrefined extra-virgin will smoke)

1 lb (450 g) baby carrots

2 shallots, cut into quarters

Lemon wedges

1 tbsp (2.5 g) chopped fresh parsley

Oil Up Them Veggies!

Water boils at 212°F (100°C) (at sea level, at least), so when your veggies hit that temp, any water in them will come shooting out, destroying the structure and resulting in weird spongy veggies. If you coat them in oil, the moisture will be kept in, resulting in luscious, perfectly formed, roasted vegetables. Think of it as sunscreen for your veggies. It's not optional!

Preheat the oven to 375°F (190°C).

Place the whole chicken breast side down on a cookie sheet to collect any errant raw chicken juices. Holding the chicken with your nondominant hand, start to cut through the chicken along the side of the backbone from the thigh end to the neck end with a pair of heavy-duty kitchen shears. Turn the chicken around and cut along the other side of the backbone, holding it from the neck. Discard the backbone or, better yet, roast it and save it for stock. Flip the chicken back over and press on the breasts to flatten the chicken. Season the chicken on both sides with salt and pepper and place breast side up.

On the stovetop, heat a cast-iron pan over medium-high heat and add the olive oil. Place the chicken breast side down (pretty side down) and cook for 5 minutes until there are some nice golden brown markings. Remove the chicken from the pan and again place on a cookie sheet to gather any uncooked juices.

Fill the pan with the carrots and quartered shallots and toss to coat with oil. Place the chicken breast side up on top of the carrots and move to the oven. Roast for approximately 30 minutes. Check it at 25 minutes with a thermometer and remove when it reads 160°F (71°C) when inserted in the thickest part of the thigh, not touching the bone. Carryover cooking will take it up to the safe 165°F (74°C) mark. Serve with lemon wedges and chopped fresh parsley.

Grape Shallot Focaccia

What I love about this recipe is making it in a cast-iron pan gives me that perfectly crispy yet moist bread.
Adding grapes and shallots keeps it interesting. Perfect blend of salty and sweet.

MAKES: 8 generous pieces

1 tsp sugar

1 (7-g) packet active dry yeast

⅓ cup (80 ml) warm, but not hot, water

2 cups (200 g) all-purpose flour

¼ tsp kosher salt

½ cup (75 g) grapes, sliced in half

2 tbsp (30 g) thinly sliced shallot

2 tbsp (30 ml) good olive oil, divided

1 tsp flaky finishing salt

2 tsp (1.5 g) dried rosemary

Dissolve the sugar and yeast in a small bowl with the warm water.

In a large bowl, combine the flour and kosher salt, and then add in the water/yeast mixture and stir to combine. When the dough comes together, switch to hand kneading and either continue to knead in the bowl or turn it out onto a floured countertop and knead for about a minute. Coat the inside of the bowl with oil and allow the dough to rise in the bowl with a kitchen towel over the top in a warm place until doubled, about half an hour.

Preheat the oven to 475°F (246°C). Toss the grapes and shallots in oil to coat.

Punch down the dough and pour 1 tablespoon (15 ml) of the oil into the cast-iron pan. Pat the dough to cover the bottom of the pan. Dimple the dough with your fingertips. Add the remaining 1 tablespoon (15 ml) of oil to the top of the dough and top with the grapes, shallots, finishing salt and dried rosemary.

Bake for 15 to 20 minutes or until golden brown and it springs back to the touch.

Remove from the pan using an offset spatula and serve with some fine olive oil and balsamic vinegar.

Indoor Grilled Marinated Steak

Living in New York City means not having much in the way of outdoor space. For me, it's probably a top-three drawback of city living. I love to cook outside. If we had an outdoor grill, I'd be the crazy lady cooking a salmon or a steak in the middle of winter, trudging through the snow. The next best thing is getting a grill pan. This is a cast-iron pan with ridges. That allows the fat to fall away (so things don't fry) and you get beautiful char marks, which also give flavor. The pan is a worthwhile investment if you miss grilling outside like I do.

SERVES: 2–4

⅓ cup (80 ml) soy sauce

¼ cup (60 ml) olive oil

¼ cup (60 ml) canola oil

⅓ cup (80 ml) lemon juice

¼ cup (60 ml) Worcestershire sauce

1 tbsp (11 g) garlic powder

½ tsp onion powder

2–4 pieces of your preferred cuts of meat, ¾" (2 cm) thick

Whisk together all of the ingredients, except for the steak, in a large ziplock bag or glass bowl. Add the steaks, being sure to cover, and marinate in the refrigerator for up to 8 hours. Longer and the steaks will start to get squishy.

Heat the grill pan over medium-high heat and lay the steak on for 3 to 5 minutes. The steak should have distinct grill marks and a dark brown sear. Flip the steaks and continue to cook until the preferred doneness is achieved, about 1 to 2 minutes for a rare steak, 3 to 5 for a medium-rare steak, 5 to 7 for a medium to medium-well steak, 9+ to ruin it. Feel free to poke it to test for doneness. The tip of most people's noses feels very much like a medium-rare steak; the firmer it is, the more well done it is.

Remember to let the steak rest before cutting into it.

Chapter 5

Let's Get Roasted

Hot, Dry and Delicious

Roasting: the process of cooking food in a hot and dry environment. It can be with super high heat for a short time or a looooooong time at low heat. Either way, remember to oil up whatever you're roasting so it keeps its shape and that if you're making something—veggies, for example—on the bottom of the pan, they won't come off that pan until they are nice and done. If you try to force them before they're ready, they'll spite you by leaving their yummy bits behind. Leave no yummy bit behind!

The Best Tools for the Job

Even if you're just cooking for one or two, it's a good idea to go with a size of at least 12 x 14 inches (30 x 35 cm) and it's nice if it comes with a rack. You can spend upwards of $200 on a roasting pan and barely ever use it because a lot of roasting jobs can take place on a sheet pan—a lot of people just bring the big boy out for Thanksgiving. I've included some recipes that put the pan to work that aren't necessarily roasting at all, it just happens to be the perfect-size pan to make crème brûlée in.

We know from previous chapters that we don't want anything to be solid stainless steel if it's going to be exposed to heat. Your best bet, just like with a saucepan, is a tri-ply construction of stainless steel, aluminum and stainless steel. Ideally the pan will be strong enough not just for oven use but also for anything that needs to get pan-seared on the cooktop before jumping into the oven. Anything flimsier than tri-ply will start to buckle and warp. Test it out in the store too. It should have big handles and I want you to imagine moving a large bird around in it, bending down and sliding it into the oven. If it's a super-heavy pan with teeny or poorly placed handles, that could spell disaster.

My favorite pan is the Sur La Table house brand pan for around $115.

PROS: It has the same construction as other higher priced pans, good solid handles and a slighter shorter side, keeping it from being cumbersome. You can easily roast your beast and then move the pan to the stovetop to reduce the pan drippings for gravy.

CONS: If you need to roast something truly giant, then you might need a bigger pan, and it stains easily like a sheet pan. A little bit of Bar Keepers Friend or Bon Ami gets any baked-on food off.

If you sprang for a pizza stone or steel, by all means leave it in the oven and place the roasting pan on top; it will help to evenly distribute the heat.

Other Tools of the Trade

PIANO WHISK: The big baller, round, balloon-looking whisk is in fact, a balloon whisk; it's all about incorporating air and volume. The piano whisk is more narrow and is more about emulsifying, like what we do with the chocolate in our Mexican Chocolate Pots de Crème recipe. If you try to whip cream with a piano whisk, it actually tastes different! Greasier, if you will. And it will take you twice as long to make it. And making a salad dressing with a balloon whisk would make you feel like a crazy person bonking that huge thing around a bowl with not much in it. You definitely need one of each. I like the stainless versions, but the new silicone versions are easy to clean and the wires don't pop out.

CUTTING BOARD: If you cook meat often, then you need to rest meat often, and that's best done on a wooden cutting board with a gutter. The Boos Blocks are gorgeous, American-made and can double as serving platters. You can get a nice one starting at $35. They are naturally antimicrobial and you can clean them with a sprinkle of baking soda and half a lemon. Scrub it in and then rinse it off. If it starts to look a little dry, then just rub some vegetable oil on it with a paper towel.

TONGS: We've already covered my love of tongs. Use them in this chapter to take the hot ramekins out of the roasting pan. Do you make preserves? I don't. I would like to learn how, but teaching sanitation for years has made me a bit gun-shy about botulism. But hey, maybe you do and that's totally cool. The jar tongs you use to sanitize ball jars are perfect for taking out ramekins.

BLOWTORCH: Ahhhhh, blowtorches—so much fun to casually whip out at a dinner party. Bear with me here, you need a blowtorch. Not a little "kitchen torch." An actual blowtorch. You can get them from the hardware store for around $45. That includes the propane tank and handy, easy-to-change trigger-action nozzle. Naturally, keep this out of reach of little hands or clumsy friends, but the power and heat they deliver is really unrivaled. You'll use it to torch sugar on banana slices, toast marshmallows in winter, heat the bottom of a cake pan if the cake doesn't want to come out, and my most common use, heat butter in the bowl of my stand mixer when I need to cream something and all my butter is cold. Also, never set it to the lock position or else the flame will stay on if you drop it. And last tip, only torch things when they aren't on a flammable surface. You'd be surprised how many students I've seen set a fire because their ramekin was on a sheet of parchment paper.

Tips for the Best Ingredients

Squash

Squash is a sport played with a tiny ball and tiny rackets by two to four players in what looks like a high-walled mental institution. It's also a delicious, hardy vegetable. Summer squash include zucchini and pattypan. The skins are delicate and edible and the seeds are usually left in. You'll want to keep them in the fridge until you're ready to eat them, and they don't tend to last beyond 5 days. Winter squash are called "winter squash" because of their ability to last the winter without suffering too much rot. These include spaghetti squash, delicata, acorn, butternut and pumpkins. The hard and thick skins are too tough to eat and the squash take much longer to cook, lending themselves to roasting beautifully. In picking a winter squash, look for unblemished skin and a uniform hardness (no squishy bruises). Winter squash are very versatile. If a recipe calls for butternut, don't hesitate to swap in an acorn squash if that's what you have on hand. The only squash that can be dramatically different is the spaghetti squash, which gets its name from the fibrous noodle-like strips you can scrape out of it after it has been cooked.

You can roast the squash either cut side up or down. Whatever is making contact with the bottom of the roasting vessel will get the most caramelization.

Squash in general are high in fiber, vitamins and minerals and should have a permanent place on your table.

Potatoes

Pick the right kind of potato! Russets and sweet potatoes are starchy. They're great for baking and frying. Red potatoes and fingerlings are both waxy. They'll hold onto their shape after cooking, so they are great for potato salad and soups (where they won't turn to mush and cloud up the soup). Yukon Gold potatoes are great for roasting and mashing.

Avoid the GREEEEN POTATOOOO! It's been exposed to too much light and has a high amount of solanine, which can give you stomach cramping, headaches and diarrhea and they taste nasty. If you have a potato that's sprouting and the sprout can be easily removed and the rest of the potato looks okay, go for it. If the potato is shriveled, you shouldn't eat it.

Maple Syrup

You're using it in moderation, so go for the good stuff! No imitation maple syrup, which is usually just colored corn syrup. Gross.

The grade system that was applied to maple syrup only referred to the color of the syrup and has since been edited so that as long as it's maple syrup it's going to be labeled Grade A, regardless of the shade. Pesticides are so rarely used on maple trees that it's also unnecessary to opt for the organic brands. It can be prohibitively expensive for independent maple farmers to obtain that certification, which in this case isn't really necessary.

The Best Techniques for Roasting

The best roasting techniques depend on the vessel you're roasting them in. If you want to roast something small, say a couple of chicken thighs and some chopped potatoes, then you'll get the best result from a no-frills half sheet pan. The lower sides will help to brown everything quickly and anything that brings a lot of moisture to the pan won't get mushy. If you're roasting large cuts of meats or roasts, then you'll want to opt for something with higher sides to help it roast more evenly. If you can put it up on a rack, even better! The air will circulate around it, cooking it nice and evenly. Keep it shallow for smaller items that need more browning.

Roasted Potatoes with Spiced Harissa Yogurt

We cut down on our cook time by blanching the potatoes first. Not just a time-saver, this step gives us a creamy, delicious inside and a crusty, roasted outside. Harissa is a North African condiment that legitimately belongs on almost everything. So much more interesting than ketchup, harissa is a hot chile pepper paste made out of roasted red peppers, serrano peppers, spices, herbs and garlic. You can find it in jars or tubes at most grocery stores now, or order from your friendly giant online retailer.

SERVES: 4–6

ROASTED POTATOES

Sea salt

1½ lb (680 g) fingerling potatoes, halved

HARISSA YOGURT

½ cup (122 g) plain yogurt

1 tbsp (15 g) harissa paste

1 tbsp (2 g) minced, fresh flat-leaf parsley, plus more for garnish

1 tsp lemon zest

2 tsp (8 g) sugar

1 tsp ground cumin

½ tsp ground coriander

½ tsp caraway seeds

1–2 tbsp (15–30 ml) oil or animal fat

Salt and ground black pepper

1 lemon, cut into wedges

Preheat the oven to 425°F (218°C).

To make the potatoes, first we will blanch the potatoes, so set aside a medium bowl of ice water. Fill a medium saucepan with water and generously salt. Add the potatoes to the cold water and bring to a boil over medium-high heat, and cook until tender, about 5 minutes. Drain in a colander and transfer to the ice water. When they are cool to the touch, fish them out and pat them dry with a paper towel.

To make the harissa yogurt, in a medium bowl, add the yogurt, harissa paste, parsley and lemon zest, and whisk to combine. Taste and adjust the seasoning with salt and pepper.

In a large bowl, combine the sugar, cumin, coriander and caraway seeds. Add the potatoes and 1 tablespoon (15 ml) of oil or rendered animal fat (duck, pork etc.), and toss to combine. If the potatoes aren't evenly covered, more oil or fat can be drizzled on top so they are well coated.

Spread the potatoes in a roasting pan. Cook the potatoes, flipping halfway through, until caramelized and golden brown, about 15 to 20 minutes. Taste and adjust the seasoning with salt and pepper.

Drizzle the harissa yogurt mixture over the potatoes and serve with lemon wedges and a flourish of chopped parsley. Be sure to flourish there; everything should be fun.

Leftovers? Smoosh up the hash with some chopped bell pepper and onion and fry it up in your cast-iron pan for some amazing harissa potato hash.

Maple-Roasted Butternut Squash

Nothing screams fall like a bunch of butternut squash. I love to cook them just sliced in half like this. It makes for a gorgeous presentation and I don't have to go through the annoyance of peeling and cubing a very slippery gourd. Roasting really brings out all of the natural sugars and creamy texture. We used miniatures here because they were freshest. Avoid bruises or squash that looks like it has wet spots.

SERVES: 4

1 whole butternut squash

Olive oil

¼ cup (60 ml) maple syrup

Salt and pepper

Preheat the oven to 350°F (176°C).

If the squash is rounded on the bottom, start by slicing off a small piece so that it will stand upright. Stand up the squash and slice down the middle. If the squash is huge, then cut it in half before attempting to cut it down the center.

Using a spoon, scrape out the seeds from the cavity.

Place the squash on a baking sheet or in a roasting pan cut side up and coat with the oil, then drizzle with the syrup and season to taste with salt and pepper.

Roast until tender, about 90 minutes. A knife should easily slide in and out.

Serve whole.

Roasted Brussels Sprouts with Garlic and Bacon

Roasting brussels sprouts is a total game changer. People who hate brussels sprouts have just never had roasted ones. The natural bitterness of the sprouts mixed with the sweet charred edges is unlike anything else. Roasting them gives us the perfect juxtaposition between the two. Adding in some sweet, smoky bacon just ups the ante even further.

SERVES: 4

3 slices uncooked bacon (or crumble a few pieces of your Candied Bacon from page 41 after the sprouts are done cooking)

1 lb (450 g) brussels sprouts, any brown root edges removed and sliced in half from top to bottom

5 cloves garlic, minced

4–6 tbsp (60–90 ml) olive oil

Salt and pepper

Preheat the oven to 400°F (205°C).

Cut the bacon into ¼-inch (6-mm) mini strips and cook until they're about 80 percent as done as you like.

Toss the sprouts, par-cooked bacon and garlic in olive oil or reserved bacon fat and spread across the bottom of a roasting pan. Roast for 15 minutes and then lightly stir with a silicone spatula. Roast for another 10 to 20 minutes or until the bacon has crisped up. Season with salt and pepper and serve.

Herb and Garlic Encrusted Lamb

This is a very classic, very fancy (very expensive) dish. Really let it get some color on the outside. It's traditional to serve lamb rare but check with your guests first! Almost everyone I know actually prefers it medium-rare and it's a pain and a shame to recook the chops after you've roasted them. You can request that your rack be frenched (the top 4 inches [10 cm] of bone are exposed, making for a prettier presentation), but I like to do it myself and then grind up the extra meat to make a sausage.

SERVES: 4

LAMB

One 8-rib rack of lamb, large fat areas trimmed off

1 tsp salt

1 tsp freshly ground pepper

Drizzle of peanut oil to coat

COATING

3 cloves garlic, grated or finely minced

¼ cup (10 g) minced fresh flat-leaf parsley

2 tsp (1.5 g) chopped fresh thyme

1 tsp chopped fresh rosemary

Pinch of salt and pepper

1 tbsp (15 ml) extra-virgin olive oil

Preheat the oven to 350°F (176°C).

To make the lamb, trim your rack of any excess fat and french the bones for presentation. Pat the rack with paper towels and season it with salt and pepper. Let it air-dry for 5 minutes (this helps the crust form).

Heat a sauté pan over medium-high heat and drizzle peanut oil to coat the bottom. When the oil begins to shimmer (when you look at it from the side and it looks like a wind is blowing across it or there are golf ball dimples), add the rack to the pan to brown it on both sides, 3 to 5 minutes.

Transfer the lamb to a roasting rack in a roasting pan (it needs to be raised in the rack to let the juices drip off).

To make the coating, mix the coating ingredients together in a small bowl and crush to combine and make into a paste. Pat the coating onto the lamb. Roast for 15 minutes and then tent with a loose layer of foil for another 10 minutes until the meat is 125°F (52°C). This is medium-rare; if you prefer a more cooked lamb, cook it until the internal temperature reads 130°F (54°C). Remove the rack from the oven and let it set, still covered loosely with the foil, for another 10 minutes to rest. Cut each rack into single chops to plate.

A Pork Shoulder of Love

It's cheap, beautiful and delicious. Bring it out to the table whole and slice it there. The skin it gets on the outside is nothing short of showstopping!

SERVES: A small army, or 8–12

---

1 head garlic

1 tbsp (15 g) salt, plus more for seasoning

1½ tbsp (4 g) dried herbes de Provence

2 tbsp (30 ml) apple cider vinegar

2 tbsp (30 ml) lemon juice

2 tsp (6 g) pepper

One 7-lb (3.2-kg) bone-in pork shoulder with skin

2 cups (470 ml) water, divided

Troubleshooting Pork Shoulder

It can be hard to tell when such a massive piece of meat is done. If yours is taking longer than you would like, then crank the heat up another 50°F (28°C) and take it up to as high as 190°F (88°C) internal temp (don't go above 200°F [93°C] or it will dry out). Don't be alarmed if it takes 2 hours to get to 150°F (65°C) internal temperature and seems to stall there for about 4 hours. It will stay around that temp until enough of the water has evaporated and then it will continue to climb up. The skin should poof up like it's been fried.

Crush the garlic cloves with the side of your knife or a bench scraper. Add the salt to the garlic and continue to crush occasionally, smearing the garlic with the side of your knife to create a paste. Move to a bowl where you will stir in the herbes de Provence, vinegar, lemon juice, salt and pepper.

Pat the pork shoulder dry. With a paring knife, cut an opening into the skin at the largest end of the roast. With your fingers, gently separate the skin in the center of the roast. Cut 1-inch (2.5-cm) deep slits into the meat and press 1 to 2 teaspoons of the garlic mixture into them. It's okay if some of the mixture comes out; the skin will hold it in place. Any leftover mixture can be spread underneath the skin. If you have the time, leave the pork shoulder in this state for an hour. The pork will come to room temperature, which helps it to cook more evenly.

Move the oven rack to the bottom. Preheat the oven to 325°F (163°C).

Place a piece of parchment paper on the roasting pan's rack and set the roast on top skin side up. Tuck another piece of parchment around the top of the pork and then cover with foil. Roast for 3 hours.

Remove the top foil and parchment and roast for another 3 hours or until a knife in the side meets little resistance. Add ½ cup (120 ml) of the water twice during the cooking time without the overhead parchment and foil. The skin will puff up like a cheese puff! It should be a beautiful dark brown (don't be put off by black pieces—they're the best).

Transfer the shoulder to a cutting board with a gutter, strain the pan juices through a strainer and discard the fat by skimming it with a large spoon. Move the roasting pan to the top of the stove and add the remaining 1 cup (235 ml) of water to deglaze over medium heat. Scrape up any brown bits on the bottom. Add the strained pan juices to the roasting pan and heat through.

Remove the skin from the pork with a slicing knife. Pull apart the pork shoulder with forks and serve with pan juices and skin. This is pretty amazing in a taco or in a sandwich or even just mounded up on the plate. The taste will just get better in the fridge.

Sweet Italian Sausage Roasted with Caramelized Onions

This is one of my go-to dishes for busy nights when there's no time to cook. It smells absolutely divine. If you know you're going to be too busy to even chop up an onion when you get home, you can do it all in advance and cover in the fridge with a splash of lemon juice to keep it from oxidizing, and then just add the sausage at the end when you're ready to roast. I like to make this on a stainless steel sheet pan with edges. I've even made small batches in my toaster oven!

SERVES: 4

1 lb (450 g) sweet Italian sausage

1 large red onion, halved and thinly sliced

5–6 cloves garlic

1 lb (450 g) fingerling or Yukon Gold potatoes, roughly chopped (optional)

Olive oil to coat

Preheat the oven to 400°F (205°C).

Run the tip of your knife around the sausages to easily peel off the casings. You can leave the sausages whole or chop them into 1- to 2-inch (2.5- to 5-cm) sections.

In a large bowl, combine the sausage, onion slices, garlic and potatoes (if using) and drizzle with a few glugs of olive oil to coat.

Arrange the ingredients on a stainless steel pan or roasting pan and roast for 20 minutes. Stir with a silicone spatula and then roast for another 15 to 20 minutes. There should be some charred onions (they're the best part!) and the edges of the sausages should be getting a little blackened. Serve with a baguette and call it the end to a good day!

Troubleshooting Stuck-on Roasted Bits

Ever go to turn potatoes over and your spatula decimates them, leaving the browned parts stuck to the bottom? It's the pits. Make sure all your veggies are coated in a thin layer of fat or oil and then let them roast until they're ready to move! Just like on the stovetop, if something isn't caramelized, it won't release from the pan. Simply cook it longer—it will release when it's done, not necessarily when you're ready. Test a few pieces on the outside and if they aren't moving freely, then pop them back in the oven for a bit. If it's apparent that there will be stuck-on bits permanently attached to your roasting vessel, then after the food has been removed, move the pan or Dutch oven to the stovetop where you can put it over some heat and add some water to deglaze it. In this case we're deglazing for the pan, but not for a sauce. It makes cleanup a snap.

Classic Crème Brûlée

Crème brûlée—such a simple, elegant dessert. It needs to be babied a bit, though. We need to bake it slowly at a low temp so the eggs set the custard instead of curdling in it. The roasting pan gives us a perfect vessel to place our ramekin(s) where we can add the perfect amount of water to ensure their slow baking.

SERVES: 4

2 cups (473 ml) heavy cream

1 vanilla bean, split, or 1 tsp vanilla bean paste or extract

Pinch of salt

6 egg yolks

½ cup (96 g) granulated sugar

4–8 tsp (16–32 g) turbinado or demerara sugar, for topping

Preheat the oven to 325°F (163°C).

Combine the cream, vanilla and salt in a saucepan over low heat until just starting to show some wisps of steam. Take the pan off the heat and allow the vanilla to steep for a few minutes. Remove the bean and rinse to save. In a separate bowl, whisk the yolks and granulated sugar together until lighter in color.

Temper the egg mixture by adding half of the hot cream mixture to the eggs while whisking (place a wet towel under the bowl if it starts to dance around the counter), then add the rest of the warm cream mixture and strain into a small pitcher or a bowl with a pouring spout.

Fill four 6-ounce (180-ml) ramekins or one giant 24-ounce (700-ml) ramekin with the custard mixture. All that matters is that whatever you put in the roasting pan is the same size so it will bake at the same rate. When filling multiple dishes, it's a good idea to only fill them up halfway at first to better gauge the amount left so nobody accidentally gets a tiny amount.

Place a kitchen towel in the bottom of your roasting pan (to keep the ramekins from sliding around) and place the ramekins on top. Move the roasting pan to the oven. While the door is still open, fill the pan with hot water halfway up the sides of the dishes. Bake for 30 to 45 minutes, or until an area the size of a dime is still jiggly in the center.

Cool them completely! Let them come to room temperature on the counter and then cool in the fridge. These keep in the fridge for 3 to 5 days.

When you're ready to serve, sprinkle each of the tops with a bit more than a teaspoon of the turbinado (sugar in the raw) or demerara sugar. There should be a complete, thin layer.

Place on a cookie sheet and fire up your torch. With the flame 4 to 5 inches (10 to 13 cm) away, pass the flame back and forth until the sugar has completely dissolved into a sweet tortoiseshell pattern. Eat as soon as possible or the sugar will begin to get soft in about an hour.

Mexican Chocolate Pots de Crème

Mexican hot chocolate makes everything better, including my wedding cake, which won on *Throwdown with Bobby Flay*. Like the crème brûlée, these bake off best in a very controlled environment and a water bath.

SERVES: 6

2 cups (473 ml) heavy cream

½ cup (120 ml) milk

2 cinnamon sticks

Pinch of cayenne pepper

5 oz (142 g) semisweet or bittersweet chocolate, chopped into small chunks

6 large egg yolks

⅓ cup (64 g) sugar

Preheat the oven to 325°F (163°C).

Add the cream, milk, cinnamon sticks and cayenne to a medium saucepan and simmer over medium heat. When steam starts to wisp around the edges, remove the pan from the heat and add in the chocolate. Allow it to melt for 1 minute before whisking with a piano whisk. Try not to incorporate any air, just stir with the whisk until the chocolate has melted and is smooth.

In a separate bowl, whisk the yolks and sugar together. Gradually whisk in the hot chocolate mixture (again using a wet towel under your bowl for stability). Strain the mixture and divide among six 6-ounce (180-ml) ramekins. Place in a roasting pan and add enough hot water to come halfway up the sides of the ramekins. Cover the roasting pan with foil and bake until a dime-size area in the center is all that is jiggly, about 50 minutes.

Remove the foil and allow to cool. Delicious served warm or cold with a dollop of whipped cream.

Chapter 6

A Tornado of Flavor

Conquering the Blender

Like most chefs, I have a soft spot in my heart for power tools, like a Wagner paint sprayer for a thin coating of chocolate and a blowtorch for some quick, concentrated heat. But the tool I use every day? My blender. Don't laugh—some models come with more horsepower than a weed whacker. Remember, though, as with any power tool, it's important to keep your fingers and toes (ew) OUTSIDE and away from the whirling attached knives. Sounds like common sense, but these babies can take away your precious phalanges before you know what's happening. Better to apply that power to the pulverizing of fruits, veggies or nuts. Pureeing your food is also a much healthier choice than juicing because it keeps all of that great fiber in your food and out of landfills.

The Best Tools for the Job

What used to be relegated to cocktail hour has become a powerful staple for the home cook.

Did you know Vitamix is responsible for the world's first infomercial? You can't go into a Costco most days without seeing someone with an ear mic giving a demo on them. And you know what? They're freaking great—the mixers, that is (people selling things make me uncomfortable).

Still, their story is pretty cool. They are an American company that started in the 1940s to help spread the word that working whole foods into your diet is healthier. To this day, Vitamix is still a family-run business.

Vita-Prep is the slightly more powerful version that is incredibly loud. They can sound like a Harrier taking off. I assume. I don't get a lot of fighter jet exposure, sadly. The extra power they have is spent mostly on cooling the motor. When any Vitamix overheats, they automatically shut off and won't turn back on until they've cooled down. These babies are a touch stronger than two horsepower and if you're running them all day, say in a restaurant or culinary school kitchen, then they are likely to heat up and will need that extra fan power. For home, though, I would definitely opt for either of the ones I have: the Vitamix 5200, which has ridiculously easy toggle controls and the taller bucket (around $450 or $100 less refurbished), or the Vitamix 7500 ($530 or about $100 less refurbished). The refurbished models still come with warranties!

Still not sold on the price tag? I get it, that's a LOT of money. The Cuisinart Hurricane Pro CBT-2000 is louder but also pretty great and comes in at around $300, and the Ninja Professional NJ600 is a pretty good deal for just $100. They are serviceable, but from a longevity standpoint, I doubt anything will last as long as your Vitamix.

A lot of blenders have removable parts to make clean-up easier. The Vitamix is not dishwasher safe (my pitcher has been run through once or twice accidentally and it's fine). The heat can cause the plastic to fog up and it's not great on the blades that are fixed in place. For the Vitamix blenders, you just fill the bucket with warm water, a squirt of soap and let it run for a few seconds. Can't really complain about not being able to stick it in the dishwasher when it's that easy to clean.

What has really brought the blender to the forefront is the number of things people have started to do with it. No more just crushing ice! Make some bread or homemade additive-free peanut butter. Do you like pancakes? I like pancakes. Go make some pancakes. The blender has become an essential power tool in our kitchen and I bet it will in yours too.

Other Tools of the Trade

BLENDER SPATULA: Both Sur La Table and Williams Sonoma have come out with great silicone spatulas that are long and narrow to fit into the base of a blender. If you're blending a lot, these are pretty important to have around and can be chucked in the dishwasher when you're done.

TEA TOWEL: Blenders are loud. Even the quietest models are still loud enough to wake a sleeping baby or grumpy spouse. Heck, I can hear my neighbors'! If you fold up a tea towel into quarters and place the mixer on top, the sound will be greatly muffled. Pull it away from the wall too; any point of contact can transmit vibrations, and vibrations = noise.

LOAF PAN: Just like cookie sheets, color matters. Go for something medium gray to light in color. A lot of the nonstick pans are just too dark; the outside of your loaf will be gorgeous but the inside raw. Something seamless will also help to keep the pan from sticking. If you generally have trouble releasing the loaf from the pan, make a saddle. Two sheets of parchment cut to fit the pan in both directions can be laid down in the pan, overhanging the sides by just an inch or two to give you a way to lift out the loaf to cool.

Tips for the Best Ingredients

Nuts

Nuts are notoriously high in fats. All of that oil can speed up the nut turning rancid. Not all nuts are created equal and some have a much higher level of polyunsaturated fats, with walnuts and pine nuts being some main offenders. Keep them in the freezer until you're ready to use them to prolong their shelf life. If your grocery store has a bulk section, then buy your nuts there; it's usually a much better deal and you can get a tiny bag if you only need a small amount for a recipe.

Cocoa

Dutch-processed cocoa is smoother cocoa with a neutral pH as opposed to non-Dutch processed, which is acidic and a little harder to dissolve. Acid reacts with baking soda, so if you're using Dutch cocoa in a recipe that calls for non-Dutch cocoa, you'll need to swap the water or milk for buttermilk or add a dash of lemon juice. The Dutch process removes a lot of the valuable antioxidants but it is *still* considered a superfood.

Baking Soda vs. Baking Powder

Ever wonder what the difference between baking soda and powder is? Or even, what the heck is baking soda? I love the stuff. It's a great natural cleaner and deodorizer. It's cheap and nontoxic. Most baking soda is mined. Nahcolite and trona are taken from the ground, usually in Wyoming or California, and turned into soda ash, which begets baking soda. The Green River Basin in Wyoming supplies up to 90 percent of the nation's soda ash. According to the U.S. Geological Survey, Wyoming alone has 56 billion tons of trona, so we should be set with baking supplies for at least the next 2,000 years.

Baking soda reacts when it comes into contact with acid—vinegar or buttermilk or lemon juice. It bubbles up and produces CO_2. This gas bubbles up during baking and makes your baked goods rise.

But what if your recipe doesn't have an acid in it? Enter: baking powder. It's baking soda with two acids snuck right in. And since the acids are in powder form, it doesn't react when it's dry. One of the acids frequently added to baking soda is either sodium acid pyrophosphate or sodium aluminum sulfate. They both need to be wet and hot, so you get a nicely delayed double reaction. This gives our protein (usually eggs) plenty of time to set up, so it stays poofy.

Fresh out of baking powder? Make your own; it's simple. Combine ½ teaspoon of cream of tartar and ¼ teaspoon of baking soda. This is equal to 1 teaspoon of baking powder. Add this and ¼ teaspoon of salt to each cup of flour if you stumble across a recipe demanding self-rising flour. If you want to make a big batch, just keep to the ratio of two parts cream of tartar to one part baking soda. It loses its potency over time, so maybe don't make more than you need and replace your baking soda every 4 to 6 months.

The Best Techniques for Blending

Blenders don't come with different blades for different jobs. It's kind of all-purpose, so the best techniques for blending apply to things that you might not think to blend that tend to drive you nuts when you want to mix them by hand—pancake or crepe batter, for example. Blending takes care of any little flour bombs left behind. Sure, protein shakes and smoothies are great, but try your blender out with some homemade nut butters and quick breads! Make it earn that giant piece of kitchen real estate it takes up.

Peanut Butter Jelly Quick Bread

Here's an extra-fun quick bread recipe. Everything whirls together in one container. I keep slices in a ziplock bag in my freezer and just pop them in the toaster oven when I need a quick snack. The slices aren't super sweet in case you're looking for a landing place for a smear of Homemade Chocolate Hazelnut Spread (page 120).

MAKES: 1 loaf

1¾ cups (174 g) all-purpose flour

1 tsp salt

1 tbsp (11 g) baking powder

1 cup (235 ml) milk

2 eggs

½ cup (96 g) sugar

1 cup (180 g) peanut butter (almond butter is also delicious)

¼ cup (60 g) jelly (any flavor)

Preheat the oven to 350°F (176°C) and coat a 9 x 5-inch (23 x 13-cm) loaf pan with cooking spray.

Stir together your flour, salt and baking powder in a medium bowl and set aside.

In this order, add the milk, eggs, sugar and peanut butter to a blender.

Begin on low speed and turn up until smooth, about 20 seconds depending on the viscosity of your nut butter. Fold the wet ingredients into your dry ingredients until combined. Pour half the batter into the prepped pan and spoon the jelly on top. Follow it with the rest of the batter and then gently swirl a toothpick to create the marbled pattern. Bake for 50 to 60 minutes or until your cake tester inserted comes out clean.

Homemade Chocolate Hazelnut Spread

Sometimes you have strawberries and only strawberries. I have no beef with strawberries, but if you happen to have some nutty chocolaty goodness for me to swirl them in before eating, well, I would appreciate that very much. This is a little less sweet than the store-bought stuff and using semisweet chocolate will up the antioxidant value. Oh, who are we kidding? This stuff is just plain yummy.

MAKES: 2½ cups (592 ml)

1 cup (170 g) hazelnuts

12 oz (340 g) semisweet chocolate, chopped (milk chocolate if you want it sweeter)

2 tbsp (30 ml) hazelnut oil

3 tbsp (24 g) powdered sugar

½ tsp vanilla extract

½ tsp kosher salt

1 tbsp (7 g) Dutch-process cocoa powder

Preheat the oven to 300°F (150°C).

Spread the hazelnuts on a sheet pan and toast for 10 minutes. They will start to scent the whole house and turn a golden brown. If the hazelnuts still have skin on them after toasting, pour them into a bowl lined with a kitchen towel (one you don't love), gather them up and rub them against one another. The skins will magically pop off.

Melt the chocolate in a double boiler or in the microwave in 15-second increments.

Add the hazelnuts to the blender and process on medium speed until they form a paste. As the hazelnuts continue to mix, stream in from the top the oil, sugar, vanilla and salt and continue to mix until smooth.

Turn the blender off and pour in the melted chocolate and cocoa powder. Blend well. Leave as is to be chunky or press through a strainer into a jar. Cover loosely and store at room temperature.

Troubleshooting Nut Butters

If your nuts don't seem to be coming together, go ahead and add 1 tablespoon (15 ml) of grapeseed or walnut oil to help lubricate it, and the next go-around, be sure to heat up the nuts to liquefy the fats so they emulsify more easily.

Simple Sweet Pea Soufflés

This soufflé tastes like spring. Frozen peas are iced almost immediately after they're harvested so they're a great alternative if it's not fresh pea season and you could use something that tastes sunny. The blender makes short work of incorporating a lot of rather chunky ingredients here.

SERVES: 4

2 tbsp (29 g) butter, divided, plus more for coating

3 tbsp (34 g) grated Parmesan or bread crumbs

½ cup (75 g) peas (thawed if frozen)

8 tbsp (60 g) grated Gruyère or Swiss cheese

1 tbsp (15 ml) olive oil

1 tbsp (6 g) all-purpose flour

½ cup (120 ml) whole milk

1 tsp chopped mint (optional)

Zest from 1 lemon

2 eggs, separated

½ tsp salt

Pinch of freshly ground black pepper

1 egg white

Preheat the oven to 375°F (190°C). Liberally butter four 6-ounce (180-ml) ramekins or one large 24-ounce (700-ml) ramekin and coat the inside with grated Parmesan or bread crumbs.

Add 1 tablespoon (14 g) of the butter to a small saucepan and heat over medium heat. Add the peas and cook until soft. Add the warm peas and grated Gruyère cheese to the blender and puree.

Place a saucepan over medium heat and melt the olive oil and the remaining 1 tablespoon (14 g) of butter. Stir in the flour with a piano whisk. This will form a roux. Stream in the milk as you continue to whisk. The mixture will suddenly become thick. Continue to whisk for 3 to 5 minutes to cook out the flour taste and reach peak thickening. Add to the blender with the pea mixture and turn on low speed. Add in the mint (if using), lemon zest, egg yolks and seasonings. Move the pea mixture to a medium-size bowl.

In a stand mixer with a whip attachment, beat the 3 egg whites until they hold soft peaks. Using a silicone spatula, stir one-third of the whipped whites into the pea mixture. Gently fold in the remaining whites in two batches.

Gently coax the mixture into the ramekins and transfer to a sheet pan. Bake until the soufflés are puffed up and golden brown, 15 to 20 minutes. Do *not* open the oven door or they will fall. Serve immediately.

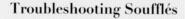

Troubleshooting Soufflés

Soufflés aren't quite as fussy as we've been led to believe. However, you can't slam any doors or check the soufflés before their time is up. The only thing puffing up the soufflés are the millions of bubbles in our egg meringue. They set slowly in the heat and even then, are so delicate that upon removal from the oven they start their descent. If you're having trouble getting the egg whites to build volume, then toss them, wash your equipment, give a quick wipe with some vinegar and start again.

Classic Spin on Macaroni and Cheese

The blender whirls around so much that eventually that friction causes heat. We can use the heat in the blender to avoid another dirty pan! Make the béchamel for your mac and cheese in the blender. It's ridiculously easy and absolutely delicious!

SERVES: 4–6

$^1/_3$ cup (76 g) butter

$^1/_4$ cup (25 g) all-purpose flour

Pinch of salt

1 $^1/_3$ cups (315 ml) milk

$^1/_3$ cup (40 g) panko bread crumbs

$^1/_8$ tsp freshly ground black pepper

$^1/_8$ tsp garlic powder

$^1/_8$ tsp dried mustard

$^1/_8$ tsp cayenne pepper

1 cup (120 g) grated cheddar cheese

2 cups (230 g) cooked elbow macaroni

Preheat the oven to 350°F (176°C). Prepare an 8 x 8-inch (20 x 20-cm) glass or stainless steel pan with a spray of cooking oil or a thin coating of butter.

Add the butter, flour, salt and milk to the blender and affix the top. Start at speed 1 and increase to top speed. Blend on high speed for 4 minutes, or until steam is pushing up through the opening.

While the blender is making the béchamel, combine the bread crumbs and spices in a small bowl and set aside.

Add the cheese to the blender and re-cover. Blend for an additional minute to melt the cheese. In a large bowl, combine the cooked elbow macaroni and sauce and stir to combine. Transfer to the baking dish.

Top the cheesy noodles with the panko mixture and bake for about 10 minutes, until the top is golden brown and bubbly.

Gazpacho

Gazpacho is all about lazy summer days, not slaving over an oven. In just 10 minutes, you could have some delicious, satisfying gazpacho in front of you. Use any kind of fresh tomato you like. This is a good time to splurge on one of those heirloom babies and, since we aren't cooking it, go ahead and use your fancy olive oil. I like the Arbequina variety, which adds a little fruity kick.

SERVES: 2

CROUTONS

1 small ciabatta loaf, cut into cubes

2 tbsp (30 ml) olive oil

Salt and pepper

GAZPACHO

1½ cups (355 ml) tomato juice, fresh or canned

1½ tbsp (22 ml) red wine vinegar

2 tbsp (30 ml) extra-virgin olive oil

1 large ripe tomato, stem removed and cut into large chunks

½ cucumber, peeled and quartered

½ small onion, peeled

½ green bell pepper, seeds removed and halved

Hot sauce

Salt and pepper

To make the croutons, toss the ciabatta cubes with the olive oil and season with salt and pepper. Toast in a toaster oven until golden brown and set to the side to cool.

To make the gazpacho, add all of the ingredients to your blender and start on slow, and then slowly increase to medium. Blend for up to 1 minute. Season the soup to taste and serve with the croutons.

Quick and Easy Frozen Margaritas

For me, the quality of crushed ice is the indicator of whether or not I bought a good blender. I feel the need to test this out frequently, much to the delight of anyone who is over.

SERVES: 4

¼ cup (60 ml) cold water

¾ cup (177 ml) tequila

¼ cup (60 ml) Grand Marnier

1 orange, peeled, seeded and halved

1 lime, peeled and halved (yay, limes are seedless!)

6 tbsp (72 g) sugar

6 cups (600 g) ice cubes

FOR THE RIM

Lime wedges, for garnish

Kosher or margarita salt (optional)

Put all of the ingredients into the container of your mixer and close the lid. Start on the lowest speed and gradually turn it all the way up. Blend for 45 seconds, pushing everything down with the tamper. If your mixer does not come with a tamper, stop every 15 seconds to scrape down.

To coat the rim, swipe a lime wedge around the edge of each glass and dip in kosher or margarita salt (if desired). Pour those margaritas and put up your feet.

Troubleshooting Margaritas

I'm a big fan of improvising when it comes to cocktails, usually because I'm out of something. No Grand Marnier? Use limoncello! No tequila? Use vodka! Just kidding! I'm not an animal—go buy some tequila if you're making margaritas. Experiment, though; try infusing it with jalapeños, which add great complexity. Don't find yourself in a rut! If things are melting too quickly, then chill the glasses you're going to use in the freezer for a bit first or keep the pitcher in the freezer after you've served the first round. With the high amount of alcohol, it won't freeze solid.

Smoothie Plan!

The most popular use for the blender is still the smoothie, so where would we be without this handy-dandy guide to build the perfect smoothie?

STEP 1: Pick a fruit. Add a handful of spinach or kale for an extra kick of nutrition without it tasting super green. Freeze them combined in a single-serving ziplock bag so you can just dump them in when you're ready to go.

STEP 2: Add liquid. My favorite is coconut water or iced coffee. Fruit juice is okay, but it translates into too much added sugar for me. Filtered water or milk of any kind works well.

STEP 3: Do you prefer a more substantial, thick smoothie? If you're not freezing your fruit, then it might feel a little runny. Thicken it up with some protein-packed nut butter, kefir, chia seeds, avocado or ice cubes.

STEP 4: Sweeten it up. A dash of stevia or a couple of dates go a long way. Maple syrup and honey both have traces of minerals and blend in beautifully.

STEP 5: Bonus round! Looking to build some muscle mass? Add a scoop of protein powder. Hemp seeds, ground flaxseeds or chlorophyll/spirulina give us a little extra glow, or add in my favorite: raw cacao. It's an antioxidant that boosts your mood and brain function. I need all the help I can get.

You always want there to be more liquids than solids. A one-to-one ratio or two parts liquid to one part solids are both great. If you consistently make too much smoothie, you can fill your cup halfway with liquid and then just add a handful of solids to get the portioning right.

Chapter 7

Dutch Ovens

The Appetizing Kind

A Dutch oven is (usually) a cast-iron pot with a lid. It's great at cooking meat in particular because it traps any steam and returns it to the pan, further developing flavors and moisture. These pots are whizzes at turning a cheap cut of connective tissue—heavy meat into something succulent and beautiful. Beyond just stews, though, a Dutch oven travels seamlessly from the stovetop to the oven to the table. Heck, it even makes bread beautifully.

The Best Tools for the Job

There aren't that many differences between brands. They are all cast iron. Some are coated on both sides with beautiful enamel. The handles should be large and comfortable. Again, get thee to a store and pick them up, see what feels good to you. The lid should be tight fitting and easy to pick up while wearing an oven mitt or holding a towel—those babies get HOT. I have a special handle that's the shape of a chicken for mine because these guys are freaking heavy and if you're at all like me, that means you're leaving them out on the stovetop, so it may as well look nice. Speaking of lids, the Staub has a lovely little design on the inside that more quickly returns steam to what you're cooking so that it's continually self-basting.

Dutch Ovens

You really can't go wrong with either Staub or Le Creuset. They both belong on wedding registries everywhere. Aesthetically, I prefer the Staub and feel like the lid is the best fitting, and I like that the sides are slightly shorter and the bottom slightly wider. The only problem is the interior is black; it can be hard to see what's going on in there, but on the other side of that coin, you don't see stains. The Le Creuset has the same level of sturdiness and the inside is usually a pale cream color, making it much easier to assess the progress you're making, but alas, it does stain and can take some real elbow grease (actually, use Bar Keepers Friend or Bon Ami) to clean. A 6-quart (5.7-L) Dutch oven from either one is around $300.

A very notable mention is the entry from Lodge! For around $65, you can get a very similar product that works amazingly well. The sides slope out a bit, so the moisture return isn't as good, but it really does work admirably well. It's definitely a great starter Dutch oven and deserves some respect.

Camp Stoves

I love to go camping. For me, camping is all about planning your next meal. Lodge makes an awesome camp stove that has feet to elevate it over hot coals. The lid is even made so that you can put hot coals on top of it too. The lid can also double as a griddle. If you walk by any campsites with one of these in view, loiter a bit, they probably have something yummy in there. This would also just be great to have if you're lucky enough to have a fire pit. Then again, I have an unnatural affinity for wanting to cook outside.

Braisers

Curious about braisers? It's just a shorter version of the Dutch oven and works just as well at breaking down tough cuts of meat. If you're not planning on using your Dutch oven to fry things in or make bread, then by all means, check them out. They're a great compromise if you're short on space.

Other Tools of the Trade

KITCHEN TWINE: It is necessary for trussing up turkeys and tying bouquet garni. You can use unwaxed dental floss in a pinch.

WOODEN SPOON: You should have more than one wooden spoon, one rounded and one with flat edges to get into the corners of Dutch ovens. Just like rolling pins and cutting boards, these do NOT go in the dishwasher. They'll get waterlogged and warp. If they start to get a little rough, feel free to sand them down and apply a little oil to bring back their natural luster.

Tips for the Best Ingredients

Onions

Onions are super hardy, so go ahead and buy the 3- to 5-pound (1.4- to 2.3-kg) bag. Store them in a cool, dry place. If you only need half of an onion, wrap the leftover in plastic wrap and keep it in the fridge. If you plan on eating it raw and don't want your date to run screaming into the night from your onion breath, soak the cut onion in cool water for 5 to 10 minutes to lessen the stinkifying effects or opt for a Walla Walla or Vidalia onion, which are naturally sweeter. The onions should be firm and have no scent when you're buying them. Yellow onions are all-purpose and have a nice balance of astringency and sweetness. White onions are sharper and have a much thinner skin. Red onions are more delicate but close to yellow onions in flavor.

If you're having difficulty with the tears when cutting an onion, you can wear some swimming goggles or aim a fan at your face. My personal favorite is to hold a mouthful of water in my mouth for the entirety of time it takes me to cut and slice the onion. It sounds bonkers, but it works for me. What also helps is a sharp blade. When we slice into an onion we break open the onion's cells, allowing the sulfenic acid to join the alliinase. They have a little chemical party that gases us as we're trying to put dinner on the table. A sharper knife means less crushing. Less crushing means less crying. Garlic also has alliinase in it—chopping your garlic and onion smaller will give your dish a MORE garlicky or oniony flavor than having large chunks floating around.

Frozen Fruits and Veggies

Frozen fruits and veggies can actually be more nutritious than buying fresh. Fresh may have had a long trip to the market and could have sat there for days, whereas frozen fruits and vegetables are typically flash frozen after being picked to maintain their fresh taste and nutritional content. What I also really love about the big bags of frozen goodness is that I have much less food waste. If you don't use that broccoli languishing in your crisper fast enough it goes slimy and you end up tossing the entire branch of it out. Frozen also gives you the opportunity to eat out-of-season foods and have them actually taste like something—hello, peas and corn! You can trust that my first picks for the week's meals will be what's in season and looks good at the market but having a go-to arsenal of fruits and veggies in the freezer stacks the deck in my favor.

Mushrooms

Mushrooms are antioxidant powerhouses and just super weird/interesting organisms. If not for mushrooms recycling plants after they die, we would be buried under several feet of debris and unable to continue our time here on earth. Mushrooms live in colonies like animals; there are colonies around Stonehenge that are so big they can be seen from airplanes. A dormant mushroom can grow after a century has passed! Some scientists think that mushrooms could survive space travel, as they are made out of chitin, the hardest naturally made substance on earth. Like I said, weird. Yeasts are also in the fungi group, without which we don't get beer and wine or leavened breads. Mushrooms only breach the surface of the ground when they are reproducing sexually. If there is a fungus among us, he or she is looking to get busy. But enough about that—how do we prepare and eat them? If I'm cooking them, they get a light bounce around a colander under a stream of cool water. It's okay to get them wet! You don't need to soak them, though. When you cook them, whether it's in a sauté pan or in a roasting pan, the mushrooms will release moisture, so you'll want to cook them with some fat. If you want to eat them raw, though, then just give them a swipe with a moist paper towel to clean.

Avoid buying the presliced plastic-wrapped mushrooms. It's too hard to see what state the guys on the bottom are in and you're stuck with that amount. Most markets have mushroom bins now, so you can pick out what and how much you want/ need. Store them in the fridge in an opened paper bag. The bag will absorb any extra moisture and the mushrooms can get some air circulation. Keep it in the crisper drawer away from cheese and onions or the mushrooms will take on some of their funky smells.

The Best Techniques for Cooking with Dutch Ovens

Dutch ovens are the best at simmering and braising, aka wet cooking. Cast iron is great at keeping your food at a consistent temperature and keeping it warm for a good long time after it's been removed from the heat. It's also great at keeping cold things cold. Chill your Dutch oven with an ice bath or by sticking it in the fridge for an hour and you'll have the perfect vessel to keep potato salad nice and cold at your next picnic.

James Beard used to line the lid of his Dutch oven with a flour paste so not even a wisp of steam could escape. If the lid of your Dutch oven is releasing steam, that's a good indicator that the flame is too hot.

Even if your Dutch oven is enamel coated, it's a good idea to give it a light coat of vegetable oil after you've cleaned it to prevent any rust in spots where the coating may have eroded.

When cooking mushrooms, be sure not to overcrowd the pan, especially in something with high sides like a Dutch oven. Give them room so that when the water releases it will evaporate quickly.

Make sure you always have a landing spot for the lid. They are incredibly heavy and unwieldy. If you're cooking multiple things in the oven and don't have room for the full height of the Dutch oven with its lid on you can turn the lid upside down and then cover it with foil to seal it. This is also a great way to store it in the cabinet so you can stack another pot on top of it.

A lot of stew recipes call for the browning of proteins before a long braise; use the lid flat on the counter to hold the raw meat while you brown it in batches. Most of them lay flat and have a lip around the edge to keep juices from making a mess.

Classic Fried Chicken

Many home cooks are wary of frying, but here's a reason to make an exception. The key is to use a pan that doesn't crowd the chicken (use two, or cook in batches, if necessary), and—most importantly—keep an eye on the heat. The chicken should sizzle merrily in the oil but it shouldn't brown too quickly or the outside will be done before the inside is fully cooked. Frying can take a surprisingly long time! Feel free to use a boneless cut of meat to cut down on time but make sure you marinate to keep it super flavorful. Don't panic if the outside gets too dark and the inside isn't to 160°F (71°C) yet; simply place the chicken on a cooling rack over a sheet pan and you can finish it in a 350°F (176°C) oven.

SERVES: 4–6

MARINADE

2 cups (473 ml) buttermilk

¼ cup (63 g) Dijon mustard

1 tbsp (11 g) onion powder

2 tsp (10 g) salt

1 tsp dry mustard

1 tsp cayenne

1 tsp black pepper

1 (3- to 3½-lb [1.3- to 1.6-kg]) chicken, cut into 8 pieces

FLOUR DREDGE

1 tbsp (11 g) onion powder

1 tbsp (11 g) garlic powder

2 tsp (5 g) dry mustard

2–3 tsp (5–7 g) cayenne pepper

1 tbsp (11 g) baking powder

5 cups (1 L) or more canola or peanut oil

To make the marinade, combine all the marinade ingredients and chicken pieces in a gallon (3.7-L) ziplock bag. Submerge the bag in water to get rid of as much air as possible and then seal it. Refrigerate it for 1 to 2 days.

To make the flour dredge, in a large bowl, whisk together the flour dredge ingredients.

Remove the chicken from the bag with a pair of tongs and place on a cooling rack set on top of a cookie sheet with edges to catch any runoff.

This is going to get messy.

Pick up individual chicken pieces and toss gently in the flour mixture to coat. Yes, some marinade will get left behind; yes, your tongs will get gunky. It will all be okay, I promise.

Let the chicken stand for 30 minutes to an hour to dry out. This is bringing the chicken to room temperature. Scary, right? Well, if we add a piece of super chilled chicken to the hot frying oil, the outside will brown beautifully but we'll have to leave it dancing in the oil a good 15 minutes before it's completely cooked. If we let the chicken hang out on a cool countertop (not sitting in the sun), some of the chill will go away and the flour dredge will form more of a crust. As the marinade seeps through the dredge, feel free to recoat it. The more coating the better.

(continued)

Classic Fried Chicken (Cont.)

Preheat your oven to 350°F (176°C). Fill your Dutch oven with 2 to 3 inches (5 to 7.6 cm) of oil. Attach a fry thermometer to the side and heat it over medium to 350°F (176°C). It's super easy to overheat your oil and it can take a very long time to bring it back down. Too hot and the outside will burn. Too cold and the crust will turn to mush. Keeping the oil as close to 350°F (176°C) as possible is key. You can always cool it down fast by adding more oil if you overshoot your goal.

Add 3 or 4 pieces of chicken to the hot oil. The temperature will drop for a moment before climbing back up. Fry for 5 minutes on each side or until a dark golden brown. Take a piece out and insert a digital thermometer. The chicken should read 160°F (71°C). There will be carryover cooking that will take it to the minimum of 165°F (74°C). If the chicken is below 160°F (74°C), and it likely will be, move the chicken back onto the rack to drain. Reheat the oil back up to 350°F (176°C) and fry the remaining chicken. Move the cookie sheet with the chicken on the rack to the oven for another 10 minutes. This will ensure that it cooks through and that the crust is extra crispy. Test it again to make sure it reaches 160°F (71°C). If you do not need to cook your chicken further, be careful not to touch the cooked chicken with anything that has touched the raw chicken, lest you run the risk of cross-contaminating it.

Dark Meat vs. White Meat

Meat is meat. Dark meat just appears darker because of the increased presence of blood vessels, which power these muscles that are constantly firing. The white meat just appears lighter because it's a muscle that isn't put to work as much. The dark meat tends to be a bit fattier and therefore more flavorful.

No Need to Knead Bread

Put that Dutch oven to work! This is probably the easiest recipe in the book. By baking our bread in a preheated Dutch oven with the lid on, we harness the steam it gives off as it cooks. This moisture will help to gelatinize the flour on the outside of your dough, resulting in an out of this world crust. By keeping the surface of the dough moist for a longer time in the oven, the yeast is allowed to eat more starch in the flour, which gives us more simple sugars. This equals flavor and a beautifully caramelized crust. You know why French baguettes are so good? Steam ovens! I don't have a steam oven, so this is the next best thing. You can bake any no-knead dough with this method. Remember, they tend to be wetter doughs.

MAKES: 1 loaf

FOR A 3.5-QT (3-L) DUTCH OVEN, DOUBLE FOR A 6-QT (5.4-L) OR LARGER

3¼ cups (323 g) all-purpose flour (I like King Arthur's Organic the best)

1½ cups (355 ml) water, at room temperature

1 tsp (7 g) active dry yeast

1¾ tsp (9 g) salt

1 cup (120 g) grated cheese or dried fruit (optional)

Vegetable oil

Combine the flour, water, yeast and salt in a large bowl and mix with a wooden spoon until everything is well blended. If you would like to add cheese or fruit, mix it in at this stage. Cover the bowl with plastic wrap and leave at room temperature for 12 to 18 hours. Or refrigerate for 24 hours and let come to room temperature before baking.

Preheat the oven to 450°F (232°C) with your Dutch oven inside. *The Dutch oven must be preheated as well!*

Remove the Dutch oven from the oven when it has preheated and lightly coat the inside with vegetable oil.

Flour your work surface and coat your hands with flour to pick up the dough. It will be sticky and feel loose. Shape it into a ball and drop it into the hot pot. With a paring knife, slice a few release cuts on the top of the dough. Replace the lid and bake for 30 minutes. Remove the lid and bake for an additional 15 to 20 minutes until the bread is beautifully browned.

Remove the bread and let it cool completely before slicing (otherwise you'll smoosh down all the nice crumb you developed and make it gummy).

Cheater Cheater Bouillon Eater: Quick Beef Stew

When there's a chill in the air and you don't have the time or inclination to cook, you can still get an amazingly flavorful beef stew on the table in under an hour. I take a few clever shortcuts here. There's a product called Better Than Bouillon. Is it as good as homemade stock? Not quite. But it's miles away from a bouillon cube. It comes in these cute little jars that you keep in your fridge. Perfect for when you realize you don't have any stock on hand. They come in beef, chicken and vegetable, and are just around $4 to $6 per jar. If I don't have homemade stock on hand, I always use this genius product.

SERVES: 4

Vegetable oil

12 oz (340 g) sirloin beef strips

2 tbsp (12 g) flour

Salt and pepper

1 large onion, chopped

3 medium-size carrots, diced

3 medium-size parsnips, diced

3 tbsp (45 g) tomato paste

2½ cups (592 ml) water

1 tsp Better Than Bouillon Roasted Beef Base (or 2½ cups [592 ml] broth)

2 medium Yukon gold potatoes, chopped into ½" (1.3-cm) cubes (about 8 oz [230 g])

2 tbsp (12 g) cornstarch mixed with ¼ cup (60 ml) water, for slurry (optional)

Place your Dutch oven over medium-high heat and coat the bottom with enough oil to cover.

Dredge the strips of meat in the flour and season with salt and pepper. Add the beef to the Dutch oven and cook until browned all over, about 5 minutes. Transfer to a cutting board with tongs. A thick layer of fond will have formed on the bottom.

Add the onion, carrots and parsnips to the pan with a pinch of salt and stir occasionally until lightly browned. If it gets too dry and begins to smoke, add ¼ cup (60 ml) of water. Add the tomato paste and cook for 1 minute. Add the water and Better Than Bouillon and stir to combine. Add the chopped potatoes. Bring to a boil, then simmer slowly for 20 minutes. Return the beef to the pot to reheat.

I prefer my stew at this consistency but if you want something thicker, use the slurry of 2 tablespoons (12 g) of cornstarch mixed with ¼ cup (60 ml) of water and stir until smooth. Add the slurry and simmer for an additional 5 minutes. The stew will need to come up to a boil to cook out the taste of raw cornstarch and activate the thickening capabilities. Serve with hearty slices of bread.

Troubleshooting the Slurry

Whenever you add cornstarch, you'll need to create a slurry. If you sprinkle in the cornstarch it will stay lumpy; by creating a quick slurry (small amount of liquid with cornstarch whisked in), it will be smooth and disperse evenly throughout the stew. If it's not thickening up you'll need to increase the heat to boiling for 30 seconds to 1 minute to fully activate the thickening power of the slurry.

Slow and Easy French Onion Soup

A perfectly caramelized onion is a thing of wonder. It's sweet and savory at the same time. It also takes forever to do it right! You can add your sliced onions to the stovetop and caramelize them from there, but to do it in a Dutch oven means you can set it and forget it for an hour or so and go do something else. Make twice as many onions as you need and freeze some for a future batch!

SERVES: 4

2 tbsp (29 g) butter

1 tbsp (15 ml) olive oil

4 lb (1.8 kg) onions, thinly sliced

1 tsp salt

3–4 cranks of pepper

2¼ cups (530 ml) water, divided

½ cup (120 ml) dry sherry

3 cups (710 ml) chicken stock or broth

3 cups (710 ml) beef stock or broth

4 sprigs fresh thyme

1 bay leaf

1 baguette, cut into ½" (13-mm) slices

2 cups (241 g) shredded Gruyère cheese

Preheat the oven to 400°F (205°C).

Add the butter and oil to a Dutch oven and melt to combine on the stovetop. Add the sliced onions, salt and pepper and stir to combine. Put the lid on and place the pot in the oven for 1 hour. After the hour, return the Dutch oven to the stovetop and remove the lid to stir the onions.

Return the lid but leave it to the side so there is a 1- to 2-inch (2.5- to 5-cm) vent. Return the pot to the oven for another hour, but check on it after 30 minutes. We want a dark caramel color. Some may get a bit black toward the edges, but don't be alarmed; it adds a depth of flavor.

If there is a great deal of moisture left in the Dutch oven, return the pot to the stovetop and stir over medium heat until the onions are no longer soggy. This will result in fond on the bottom. Stir in ¼ cup (60 ml) of the water to deglaze the pot, scraping up the yummy, baked-on bits with a wooden spoon. The onions will get very dark.

Stir in the sherry and continue to cook on the stovetop until it reduces down to looking dry again.

Stir in both stocks, the remaining 2 cups (470 ml) of water, thyme, bay leaf and another pinch of salt and pepper. Bring to a boil and then reduce the heat to low, cover and allow it to simmer for 30 minutes.

Discard the thyme sprigs and bay leaf. Taste and season.

Portion the soup into heatproof bowls and float slices of baguette on top. Loosely mound the shredded Gruyère on top and broil for 3 to 5 minutes or until the Gruyère is bubbly and darkened in spots. With oven mitts, carefully serve!

The Sunday Sauce *(Bolognese Sauce, aka Ragù)*

This is a special treat. Having this kind of time to hang around as a pot bubbles lazily away in the corner is a real luxury nowadays. If you have a larger Dutch oven, then definitely double the recipe. It makes for a killer lasagna and freezes like a dream. Or gift a jar to a friend you owe a favor to. Keep a spoon handy to taste and season as you go along.

SERVES: 6

1 tbsp (15 ml) vegetable oil

3 tbsp (43 g) butter

½ cup (75 g) chopped onion

½ cup (75 g) chopped celery

½ cup (75 g) shredded carrot

1 lb (450 g) ground meat (either all 80% ground beef or half and half beef and pork)

Salt and pepper

1 cup (235 ml) whole milk

¼ tsp freshly grated nutmeg

1 cup (235 ml) dry wine (either color)

1½ cups (241 g) crushed tomatoes, ideally San Marzano

1 lb (450 g) pasta (Hey! Check out the fresh pasta recipe on page 26.)

Add the oil and butter to your Dutch oven and heat over medium heat. Add the onion and cook while stirring until it becomes translucent, about 5 minutes. Add the celery and carrot, cooking for an additional 2 minutes until they are all coated with oil and beginning to soften.

Add the ground meat to the vegetables with a large pinch of salt and a few cranks of pepper. Allow the meat to cook for at least a minute before breaking it up with a wooden spoon and continuing to cook until all the meat is brown. Pour in the milk and grated nutmeg and simmer until it appears dry, about 5 minutes.

Add the wine (it really doesn't matter if it's red or white, I promise. Just make sure it's not sweet) and let it simmer until it too has evaporated. Add the tomatoes to the pot—careful, they splatter—and thoroughly stir to combine. When the sauce begins to bubble, lower the heat to a slow simmer and cook uncovered for 1 to 3 hours. It's delicious at 1 hour but even more decadent after 3.

If the sauce begins to look too dry or sticks to the bottom of the pan, add ¼ cup (60 ml) of water and stir to combine as necessary. Skim any pools of fat from the surface with a spoon or ladle and discard.

Serve with a hearty homemade pasta like pappardelle or a box of dry rigatoni.

Dutch Oven Mushroom Pea Risotto

I mentioned briefly in the cheater beef stew recipe that the cornstarch needs to cook completely to thicken and get rid of its starchy taste. The same holds true for risotto. If you leave a cup of rice in a bowl of cold water overnight, *nothing* will happen. Only the heat can activate the starches and get everything moving. But does it really need all that stirring? No, as a matter of fact, it doesn't. A quick, hearty stir at the end will activate all the rice's starches and give you that risotto creaminess that we all love.

SERVES: 4

1½ cups (316 g) Arborio rice

5 cups (1.2 L) warm chicken stock, divided

1 tbsp (15 ml) extra-virgin olive oil

4 tbsp (57 g) butter, divided

1 shallot, minced

10 oz (283 g) mushrooms of your choice, stemmed and roughly chopped

2 tsp (10 g) salt, plus more as needed

1 cup (100 g) grated Parmesan cheese

½ cup (120 ml) dry white wine

1 tsp pepper

1 cup (151 g) frozen peas

Preheat the oven to 350°F (176°C).

Place the rice and 4 cups (945 ml) of the chicken stock in a Dutch oven. Cover and bake for 45 minutes.

In a shallow pan, heat the oil and 1 tablespoon (15 g) of the butter on the stovetop over medium heat and sauté the chopped shallot until translucent, about 5 minutes. Add the chopped mushrooms and a pinch of salt and sauté until the mushrooms begin to get some color and lose most of their moisture.

After 45 minutes, remove the Dutch oven from the oven and place on a burner. Most of the liquid will be absorbed and the rice will have just a slight chew left to it. Add the remaining 1 cup (235 ml) chicken stock, Parmesan, wine, remaining 3 tablespoons (42 g) of butter, salt and pepper and stir vigorously for 3 minutes. Add in the peas and cooked mushroom-shallot mixture and stir to combine. Serve hot.

Perfect Poached Pears

These pears floating in a jar are a perfect gift and an elegant dessert. Any leftover poaching liquid mixed with some hooch makes the most amazing hot toddy ever. Have fun with the add-ins and use your imagination.

SERVES: 4

4 Bartlett pears, peeled and cut in half from top to bottom

1 lemon, halved and juiced

1 (750-ml) bottle white wine

¾ cup (144 g) sugar

1 tsp peppercorns

1" (2.5 cm) piece fresh ginger, smashed

3 cups (710 ml) water

1 cinnamon stick

Remove the seeds from the pears with a melon baller. Cut a small V in the pear halves to remove the fiber coming down from the stem if you see it. Place the pears in the Dutch oven. Squeeze the lemon directly over the pears and then toss in the spent lemon peel. Add the wine, sugar, peppercorns, ginger, water and cinnamon stick.

Place the Dutch oven over medium heat and top with a cut circle of parchment paper that will lightly cover the top of the pears. This will keep a lot of the moisture in the pan while allowing a controlled amount to escape and keeps the pears from coming out of the liquid. Do not let the pot start to boil or the pears will be destroyed in the onslaught of bubbles. It should just be bubbling up sporadically.

Cook for about 25 minutes or until a cake tester in a pear can slide in without resistance. Using a spider or slotted spoon, remove the pears and set to rest on a cooling rack. Return the cooking liquid to a boil and reduce by one-third, about 15 minutes. Allow the pears and liquid to cool separately.

Store the pears in the poaching liquid or serve at room temperature. Remember, extra poaching liquid + brandy to taste = a cure to whatever ails ya'.

Chapter 8

You Spin Me Right Round Baby, Right Round

Stand Mixers 4 Life

Back in 2003, Jim and Karen Ralston gave me a life-changing wedding present: the KitchenAid Stand Mixer. This shiny beauty was the first serious piece of kitchen equipment I had and I started to spend serious time in the kitchen.

The Best Tools for the Job

The KitchenAid brand has continued to grow and branch out and has a handy port for attachments. No matter when you bought your stand mixer, there's a portal on the top that you can plug myriad things into. There are spiralizers, pasta makers, meat grinders and more. They are pricey but if you think you'll use them, they make short work out of some complicated things. Mixer choice is very personal, but here are my suggestions.

For the Sometimes Baker

Baking 3 to 5 times a month – KitchenAid KHM926 handheld mixer, $100

PROS: Small and powerful. Storage is a snap.

CONS: Bigger jobs like bread kneading will need to be done by hand.

For the Frequent Baker

Baking 4 to 20 times a month – Breville BEM800XL at $300 or KitchenAid Pro 6400 at $550

PROS: You can buy extra bowls for both, which makes big baking days a breeze. They are both powerful and should give you at least 10 years of use.

CONS: If all you do is make bread, then the motors will eventually burn out on you. These both take up significant counter space.

For the Frequent Bread Baker

Bosch Universal Plus Mixer, $500

PROS: This baby can make up to 15 pounds (6.8 kg) of dough at a time. The controls are super simple and with the motor being below, it's easy to add ingredients to the bowl without making a huge mess.

CONS: It's also a counter hog and slightly more expensive.

For the Semiprofessional/Professional

Everyday use, need to make large batches – Ankarsrum Original Stand Mixer, $700

PROS: The 7-liter stainless steel bowl makes short work of big doughs and the motor housing in the base gives you better torque. Loads of available accessories for all you sausage and pasta makers out there, too. Oof, $700. If you're making upwards of 30+ loaves a bread a week, then I recommend the Häussler brand, an investment at around $700+.

CONS: The price.

Think about the weight of the mixer and where you're going to be keeping it.

Don't buy a mixer based on wattage. That's just the power that it's going to use, not the power it exerts. Take a look at the height of the beaters or whisk attachments; if they don't go up to the top of the mixing bowl, then you'll never be able to effectively mix the full bowl amount.

KitchenAid is the standard we hold most mixers to and here are some important tips to get the most out of yours.

To adjust the height of the beater: lift the head up, and you should see a rectangle hole with a flat-head screw. Turn the screw counterclockwise or left to raise the beater. Turn the screw clockwise or right to lower the beater. Each time only turn the screw about a quarter turn at a time and test again. There should only be room for a dime to pass between the bowl and the beaters.

On bowl-lift models, your stand mixer is adjusted at the factory, so the flat beater just clears the bottom of the bowl. If, for any reason, the flat beater hits the bottom of the bowl or is too far away from the bowl, you can correct the clearance easily. The screw is located directly between the arms that hold the bowl. To move the bowl further down, screw to the right. To reduce the clearance of the bowl (bring it up), turn it to the left. Test it between adjustments.

Other Tools of the Trade

EXTRA SMALL BOWL: The KitchenAid isn't great at small jobs. One or two egg whites and you're almost better off doing it by hand, but lo and behold, the KN3CW 3-quart (2.8-L) Mixing Bowl & Combi-Whip is for use with 5- and 6-quart (4.5- and 5.4-L) bowl-lift KitchenAid stand mixers. It has multiple holes, so it will fit either mixer. Guys, this is huge. Well, technically it's small, but it's awesome! Totally worth the $60 price tag. If you make mousse or separated egg foam cakes, this is a huge time-saver and convenience.

SILICONE SPATULA: Silicone spatulas won't melt up to around 800°F (427°C). You can usually pull off the business end and dishwash them (hand wash the wooden handle to keep it from getting too rough or warping). They won't chip, crack or dry out. It's a good idea to have a few on hand in various sizes, especially if you want to color multiple batches of frosting. You can get themed ones at fancy kitchen stores after most holidays (honestly, most of the year I'm working with my Halloween spatulas; they make me happy). They'll run you $4 to $15 dollars each.

PIPING BAGS: This is a tricky one. I try to be environmentally conscious, but when it comes to piping bags I usually buy disposable ones from Ateco. You can use a zip-top bag in a pinch, but they can't really take much pressure. The canvas bags are lovely but they are difficult to clean really well. If there's an iota of buttercream left, it can rot or ruin whatever you're making next. If you insist on the canvas bags, soak them in a hot dish soapy bath with a few capfuls of vinegar. The cost is $5 for a dozen disposable bags or $5 for a reusable canvas bag.

Tips for the Best Ingredients

Egg Whites

We've already talked about eggs, but for things like meringues or Swiss buttercream, we just need the whites. I prefer to use fresh whites, separating them myself and using the yolks to make a pudding (or tossing them, they don't keep as long as whites do). I have also used the quarts of whites available in most grocery stores. These are pasteurized to a higher degree, which starts to break down the egg's proteins. We need these proteins to streeeetch and support the giant bubble structure that is our meringue. Do they work? Yes, and since they're very pasteurized, they're very safe to eat. Do they work as well as fresh whites? No, no they don't. You'll get about 15 to 20 percent less volume. It's not a deal breaker, just something to consider when you're making your meringue.

Cake Flour

Cake flour has a protein content of about 8 percent, while all-purpose flour is around 10 to 11 percent. Using a flour with a lower protein content keeps the cake from developing too much gluten and getting tough. Make sure that you just buy cake flour if the recipe calls for it and NOT self-rising cake flour. That already has the salt and baking soda/powder added in and will wreck your cake and make a mess in your oven. Don't have any cake flour on hand? Measure out what you need with all-purpose flour, then take away 2 tablespoons for every cup. Then add 2 tablespoons (19 g) of cornstarch for every cup measured. Give it a good whisk and it's ready to use.

The Best Techniques for Using a Mixer

Stand mixers are the best to use when you have a large volume or something that would offer a lot of resistance where a handheld mixer just wouldn't do. You also can't beat the efficiency of a stand mixer when it comes to making a whipped cream or meringue. Making a meringue by hand just once will convince you that this powerhouse is worth it. It's also great to quickly mix together meatballs so that your hands don't heat up and start to break down the fat. You also can't beat the bread hook when it comes to making large loaves of bread. Sure, you could knead them by hand, but having it all contained in a cool metal bowl is quite the time (and mess) saver.

Happy Birthday Cake

This is a high ratio white cake. High ratio refers to the amount of sugar and fat in relation to the flour. It's most similar to boxed cake mix flavor, without all the preservatives and artificial colors. It does not rise as high as other cake batters, so be sure not to overfill your pan, or the cake will get gummy. This works with a hand mixer or stand mixer. Either one, but you'll definitely want to use a mixer!

MAKES: Two 9-inch (23-cm) cakes

2 cups (473 ml) milk

12 egg whites

1 tbsp (15 ml) vanilla extract

1 tsp almond extract

5 cups (450 g) cake flour

1 tbsp plus 1 tsp (15 g) baking powder

2 tsp (10 g) salt

4 cups (766 g) sugar

1½ cups (340 g) butter, cubed, at room temperature

Preheat the oven to 350°F (176°C). Butter and flour two 9-inch (23-cm) cake pans.

In a bowl, combine the milk, egg whites and extracts, and set aside.

In the bowl of a stand mixer, add all of the dry ingredients and the sugar. Mix on low speed to combine. Add the butter cubes and continue to mix on low speed until the mixture resembles cornmeal. Add half of the egg white/milk mixture and mix until well combined and thick, about 1 minute. Scrape down the bowl.

Mix in the remaining liquid and continue to mix, stopping frequently to scrape down the sides of the bowl. Continue until well mixed, approximately 1 more minute. Pour the batter into the prepared pans; the batter should not go up more than halfway.

Bake for 20 to 30 minutes or until a cake tester inserted comes out cleanly and the surface is a golden brown that bounces back to the touch. The cake should pull away slightly from the sides of the pan. Wait 5 minutes and then invert onto a cooling rack.

Troubleshooting Cake Batter

Did you get a lot of large holes in your finished cake? That's called "tunneling" and it comes from overmixing your cake batter. Sure, cake flour has less gluten than all-purpose flour, but it's still flour! There's still plenty of gluten in it and you need to treat it gently to avoid overdeveloping it and ending up with these annoying pockets. Try finishing it by hand with a rubber spatula next time.

Difficulty getting it out of the pan? Make sure you generously coat the pan with a nonstick flour spray specifically for baking or brush plenty of room-temperature butter and make sure it all gets coated with a nice dusting of flour. Still stuck? It happens! Break out that trusty blowtorch, invert the pan and give it a few passes. No torch? Heat the bottom of the cake tin over the stovetop and then invert it and give it a few hearty taps to release it.

You'll want to remove a cake from its pan as soon as possible unless it's in a super-shallow sheet pan; otherwise, the hot steam will make the edges go gummy.

Swiss Meringue Buttercream

Unlike the cloyingly sweet grocery-store cupcake frosting, Swiss meringue is light and fluffy and won't make your teeth run screaming out of your mouth. After it's made, feel free to flavor it with seedless preserves, fruit curds, extracts or chocolate. This is the recipe I've been using for the last 15 years for all my cakes. You can use a hand mixer for this but be warned, you'll be standing with it for about 10 minutes.

MAKES: Enough for a 9-inch (23-cm) cake

12 egg whites

3 cups (600 g) sugar

2½ lb (1.1 kg) butter, cut into cubes (ideally at room temperature)

In the bowl of an electric mixer or in a large mixing bowl, whisk together the egg whites and sugar and place over a pot of simmering water. Whisk until the temperature of the eggs reaches 130°F (54°C). It will feel like very warm bathwater. Be careful, the sides of the bowl are likely very hot. Carefully move the mixing bowl onto your stand mixer or onto a dry towel if using a hand mixer.

Start whipping on medium-high speed until the meringue has at least doubled in volume, has cooled down to room temperature and is holding a stiff peak. Test the temperature of the whipping whites with your finger—if it's still warm, it will melt the butter, deflating all of the volume. Continue whipping until it's room temperature or make sure the butter you add is cool.

Begin adding the butter to the whipping meringue, continuing to whip and adding butter until complete. Increase the speed of your mixer until the buttercream is light and smooth. Flavor as you wish.

This buttercream may be stored in an airtight container in the fridge or frozen. Let the buttercream come to room temperature before attempting to use. In case of a buttercream emergency, get out the blowtorch and gingerly heat the outside of your bowl for 5 seconds every 30 seconds until it all comes back together.

Troubleshooting Buttercream

OMG, it looks like curdled milk! It's okay, the temperature was off and the emulsion has begun to separate. There's a lot of water in egg whites and in butter; when it separates from the fat it might start to look like a curdled mess. It will come back, I promise. Continue to mix the heck out of it and it will re-emulsify.

Ginger Citrus Pound Cake

Pound cakes have been around forever. All you really need to know is a ratio. One pound (454 g) each of sugar, butter, eggs and flour. That's it. Of course, we soup them up and make them our own by playing with the ratio and adding fun ingredients. What I love about them is that you can change it up by how you make it. Is the butter melted or creamed? It makes a huge difference. When we blend together sugar and eggs in a mixer, we "cream" it. Some of the sugar dissolves but the rest of it forms tiny air pockets in the butter so that when it bakes they blow up like tiny balloons, giving us a lighter cake, even though it's still a pound cake.

MAKES: 1 loaf

CAKE

2 tbsp (19 g) lemon or lime zest

1 cup (192 g) granulated sugar

3 tbsp (43 g) grated ginger

1 cup (99 g) all-purpose flour

1 tsp baking powder

Pinch of salt

¼ cup (60 ml) milk

1 tsp vanilla extract

½ cup (115 g) butter, at room temperature

2 eggs

2 tbsp (30 ml) lemon or lime juice

GLAZE

3 tbsp (44 ml) fresh lemon or lime juice

1 cup (130 g) powdered sugar

Lemon or lime zest, for garnish

Preheat the oven to 325°F (163°C) and generously butter and flour a loaf pan or a Bundt pan.

To make the cake, add the zest to the granulated sugar and mix by hand. Then add in the ginger.

In a large bowl, whisk together the flour, baking powder and salt.

Stir together the milk and vanilla in a small bowl and set to the side.

In a large bowl or stand mixer, cream the butter and citrus sugar until light and fluffy, about 4 minutes. Add the eggs in one at a time and fully incorporate until the mixture again looks light and fluffy.

Alternate between adding the flour and milk mixture to the butter mixture until it's just incorporated. Add the citrus juice at the end.

Spoon the batter into your pan and bake until a cake tester comes out clean, about 45 minutes to an hour. Allow to cool on the counter for 5 minutes and then invert onto a rack to cool.

To make the glaze, slowly add the citrus juice to the powdered sugar and stir. For a thin glaze, add more juice; thicker, add more powdered sugar.

Drizzle it over the top of the cake and garnish with a little more zest.

Luscious Lemon Curd Pavlovas

This is the perfect recipe for when you're meeting your husband's Aunt Astrid in Norway and she knows you're a chef and you're jetlagged but still want to do something moderately impressive. The juxtaposition of the sweet and crispy yet chewy meringue, with a burst of lemony tartness, all tempered with a layer of creamy whipped cream makes this my absolute favorite dessert. Be sure to really clean your whips. Any bit of leftover fat will keep them from gaining any volume.

SERVES: 6–8

PAVLOVA

4–5 egg whites, at room temperature

1 tsp cream of tartar

Pinch of salt

1 cup (192 g) sugar

½ tsp vanilla extract

WHIPPED CREAM

1 cup (235 ml) heavy cream

1 tbsp (12 g) sugar

LEMON CURD

½ cup (120 ml) fresh lemon (or lime or passion fruit) juice

½ cup (96 g) sugar

3 eggs

6 tbsp (86 g) butter, cut into cubes

Berries, for garnish

Preheat the oven to 180°F (82°C). Prepare a sheet pan with a piece of parchment or a Silpat.

To make the pavlova, add the egg whites, cream of tartar and salt to the bowl of your mixer and beat with the whisk attachment on medium-high speed until bubbles start to form. As it continues to whip, slowly stream in the sugar. Continue to beat until firm, shiny peaks form, about 2 minutes.

Remove the bowl and fold in the vanilla. Pile the meringue onto the cookie sheet in 6 to 8 round forms. They should look like round, flatish pillows. Bake for 1½ to 2 hours. Allow the meringues to cool at room temperature. Slice off a little cap on each one.

To make the whipped cream, using a balloon whisk or your stand mixer, beat the heavy cream and sugar until medium peaks form. If you overwhip the cream, it will start to look grainy. Add an additional tablespoon (15 ml) of cold cream and gingerly stir it in with a rubber spatula to bring it back to its perfectly whipped, creamy self.

To make the lemon curd, whisk together the juice, sugar and eggs in a heavy saucepan. Add in the butter and stir with a wooden spoon over medium-low heat until the curd is nappant (fancy word for holds a line when you run your finger across it without dripping). This takes about 6 minutes. Strain the curd into a bowl and allow to cool at room temperature for about an hour.

Serve the pavlova with the lemon curd hidden in the center of the meringue and the whipped cream on top. Garnish with berries.

Whipped Coconut Milk Ganache

Who knew you could get such a decadent, creamy ganache with no dairy! Be extra careful when mixing this! If you don't stop right when it's the consistency you want, it will go grainy on you. This is amazing between cookies or as a cake layer.

MAKES: 3½ cups (825 ml)

1½ cups (355 ml) full-fat coconut milk (shake the can or whisk to make homogenous)

2 cups (360 g) dark chocolate, chips or chopped

Pinch of salt

In a saucepan, heat the coconut milk until the edges start to bubble. In a separate bowl, pour the steaming milk over the chopped chocolate and pinch of salt. Let it do its thing! The hot coconut milk is melting the chocolate—if we start stirring right away, it will cool down the milk and our chocolate won't melt all the way.

After 2 minutes of staring at the bowl, slowly begin to whisk in the center of the bowl; as the chocolate incorporates, widen your stirring area until the entire bowl looks like chocolate soup. Taste it with a clean spoon for uh . . . quality control.

If you would like to use it as a glaze, now is the time. If you would like to use it as a cake filling, allow it to cool for 2 to 3 hours until the consistency is more spreadable than pourable.

Use any leftover ganache to dip strawberries in or eat it in the corner when nobody is looking.

All Hail the Challah

I love foods that can do double duty. If you have challah in the house, you have the perfect base for bread pudding, killer French toast, decadent grilled cheese or heck, even a sandwich. If you don't have a stand mixer for this, then I recommend kneading it by hand. It will take about 10 minutes but you'll get a nice workout in!

MAKES: 1 large loaf or 2 small loaves

2 tsp (14 g) active dry yeast

1 cup (235 ml) warm water

4–4½ cups (400–450 g) all-purpose flour

¼ cup (48 g) sugar, plus a pinch

2 tsp (8 g) salt

2 eggs

1 egg yolk

¼ cup (60 ml) extra-virgin olive oil

1 egg plus a pinch of salt, whisked, for egg wash

Pearl sugar, everything bagel seasoning or sesame seeds, for topping (optional)

In a small bowl, sprinkle the yeast over the water and add a pinch of sugar. Stir to dissolve and let rest for 5 minutes until it starts to bubble.

Whisk together the flour, sugar and salt in the bowl of a stand mixer.

Add the eggs, yolk and oil to the center of the dry ingredients and begin incorporating with a wooden spoon. With a dough hook attachment, begin mixing the dough and pour in the yeast mixture, being careful to scrape all the yeast into the mixing bowl. Knead for 6 to 8 minutes on low speed. If after 8 minutes the dough sticks to your fingers like gum, add 1 tablespoon (6 g) more of flour and mix for an additional minute. The dough should be soft and smooth.

Oil a large bowl and place the dough in the center. Cover with a towel or oiled plastic wrap and let sit in a warm place until it has doubled in size, about 2 hours.

With a bench scraper, separate the dough into 3 pieces and roll into ropes. Squeeze them together at one end and braid down the rest of the way, squeezing together at the other end and tucking the ends underneath. Place the completed braid on a parchment paper–lined cookie sheet and let it rise for another hour.

Preheat the oven to 350°F (176°C).

Brush the challah with the egg wash and bake for 30 to 35 minutes. I sprinkled the one here with pearl sugar, but you could also use everything bagel seasoning or sesame seeds. The challah should be deeply brown, even in the crevices. Let the challah fully cool before cutting.

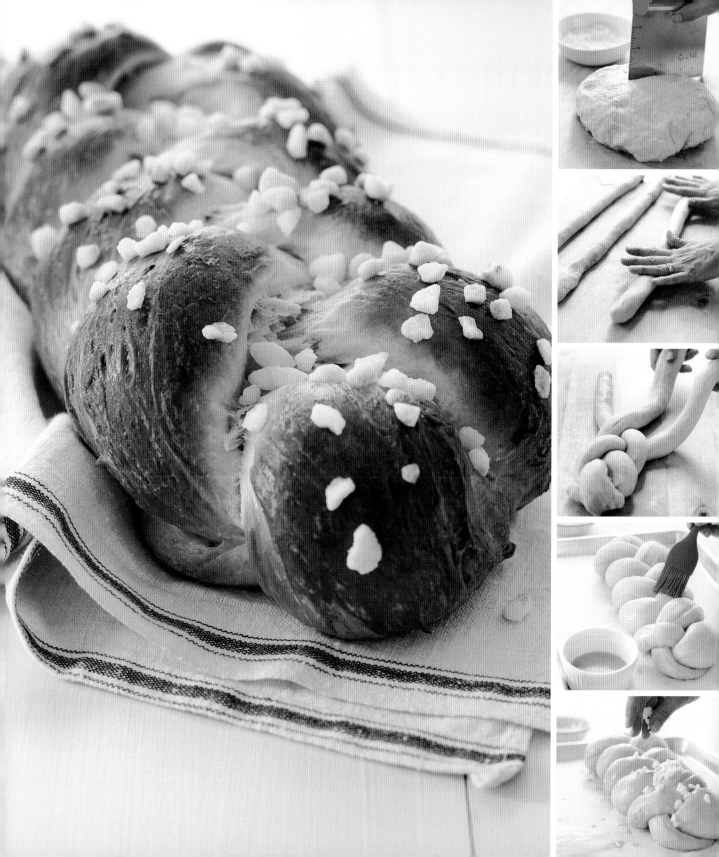

Chapter 9

Under Pressure

Pressure Cookers

At sea level, we are exposed to 14.7 pounds (6.6 kg) of atmospheric pressure per square inch (2.5 cm). If you go mountain climbing, there's less gravity holding down the atmosphere around you; that's why we get altitude sickness if we're not used to it and why a lot of climbers bring along canisters of breathable air. If you live on Mount Everest or even in Denver, you've experienced this. Maybe not the climbing part but the whole "food cooks differently up here" part.

The Best Tools for the Job

You'd be hard-pressed to find anyone in the Andes NOT cooking with a pressure cooker. At sea level, water boils at 212°F (100°C); on Everest, water boils at 160°F (71°C). It takes way too long to get anything on the table. Introduce a pressure cooker, though, and dinner cooks in a fraction of the time!

Pressure Cooker

As water turns to steam, it takes up more physical space, which creates pressure. The more pressure, the hotter the water can become before boiling. This allows us to take what is inside the pot above 212°F (100°C). This is physically impossible to do without a pressure cooker. It feels dangerous! It's really not—pressure cookers are made with strong seals and most nowadays have a secondary valve to prevent too much pressure from building up.

If you're using a simple stovetop version, you'll hear a whistle—this means that you've reached maximum pressure and pressure is escaping through the safety valve. You can just lower the heat to hear a slight whistle to know it's working.

Multi-Cooker

Over the last few years an amazing crop of multifunction small appliances have hit the market: the Instant Pot, Breville Fast Slow Pro Multicooker and the Fagor LUX Multicooker, among others. They are all pretty amazing machines. If you're in the market for a slow cooker, I recommend springing for a multi-cooker. So far my favorite is the Instant Pot.

PROS: They have a handy digital readout and come with a lot of preprogrammed options. You can cook food slowly just as easily as you can pressure cook it. Cheap! In some cases, they are less expensive than a nice single-purpose pressure cooker. They come standard issue with a basket, which makes the retrieval of food super simple. They've become so popular that a whole string of great cookbooks just for them have popped up. When I brought mine home, a stranger yelled across the street, "Is that your first Instant Pot? You're gonna friggin' love it!" Did I mention I live in Brooklyn? I love Brooklyn.

CONS: Despite their "sear" function, it's still better to brown meat on the stovetop. You are better off with a shallower vessel to get a really nice sear on meat; doing it at the bottom of a pot creates a lot of trapped steam, which is no help at all and it's also awkward to manage the checking and moving of pieces. These pots are also big, taking up a lot of counter space and electricity requiring a conveniently placed outlet.

Not up for another electric device? I get that. A standard stovetop pressure cooker gets the same job done. I like the Presto 8-Quart Stainless Steel Pressure Cooker for around $50.

Other Tools of the Trade

Cutting Boards

My preferred cutting board is a slab of maple that was a gift from a graduating class at culinary school. I use it for everything, the wood doesn't overly dull my knives and it looks great. But for raw meat, I only use plastic. Here's why you need one of each.

Wooden

PROS: Self-healing—to a point, but the nature of wood will swell up when it gets wet, so after washing it doesn't look as scratched. They are super easy to refinish if it does start to look junky. Just pass a fine sandpaper over it a few times and it's virtually new! Clean them off with some vinegar and recondition with some canola oil and they're pretty enough to bring to the table.

CONS: There were some studies in the 1990s that said wooden boards are naturally antimicrobial. I don't really buy that but I can say that wooden boards are slightly harder to sanitize. You don't want to subject them to scorching hot water—the grain will rise and become rough and if it's a bamboo board, forget about it, it will disintegrate or come back curved like a canoe.

Plastic

PROS: Cheeeeeap cheap cheap. Like, seriously dollar store cheap. And super easy to clean. Dishwashing to sanitize is a breeze and won't negatively affect them. You can color code them to help avoid cross-contamination. They are light and easy to store. I have a file folder organizer under my sink where I keep them all vertical for easy grabbing.

CONS: They are kind of ugly and rarely come with any kind of gutter. Juices run off the sides very easily and can be messy. They also aren't very kind to knives and once they are scratched you'll see it forever.

Both types of cutting boards can slide around dangerously on the countertop. Put a moist paper towel underneath to keep it in one place.

Buy one of each. I love Boos Block boards for my wooden ($25 to $200) and IKEA's set of 2 plastic cutting boards for just $15.

Glass cutting board?

Terrible, terrible idea. Weighs a ton, destroys your knife and ridiculously heavy. Just no.

Peeler

Get thee a Y-shaped Kuhn Rikon peeler. These feel the most natural in your hand and are safer to use than the traditional shape. They come in bright, cheery colors and you can pick them up for around $4 each. I buy a multi-pack every year to separate into stocking stuffers. Spring for a couple for yourself to have on hand.

Strainer

I use this for sifting flour, adding powdered sugar to the tops of desserts and straining stock. It's earned a place hanging right next to my sink it's used so much. You'll want one with a loop on the far end. This isn't just for hanging but for latching onto the edge of your bowl so you can pour whatever is being strained without having to hold it. Rosle makes a beautiful one for $20 and the Sur La Table house brand is also pretty great and around $20. Chef's Planet has recently released a clip-on strainer that you attach to the side of a pot that works great for draining pasta. It's around $15 and I've been using it more than I thought I would.

Tips for the Best Ingredients

Fresh Herbs

It can feel like a losing battle bringing home fresh herbs. They wilt faster than wildflowers! As soon as you bring them in, float them in a bowl of tap water for a few minutes to clean. Lay the wet herbs on a paper towel and then wrap them up with that damp paper towel. Then place these herbs in a labeled ziplock bag in the fridge and you should get about a week of life from them.

Bones

Hold on to your leftover bones! When we make stock, we're pulling all the gelatin and marrow and scrappy deliciousness left behind. There's a reason why meat is so much tastier when it's made with the bone in. The bone has flavor. Dogs aren't just chomping on them for kicks! I like to roast my bones before I make a stock to give an extra layer of flavor, but it isn't necessary. Don't be shy about asking your butcher for soup bones either. They'll be excited to unload them!

The Best Techniques for Using a Pressure Cooker

Follow instructions! You're cooking with a high temperature. The newfangled machines have lots of safety backups, so familiarize yourself with them.

Always check the rubber gasket around the lid of your pressure cooker to make sure it isn't cracked or wearing out. Avoid overfilling your pot; it's not good to have something block the gasket. It shouldn't be more than two-thirds full, or if it's rice, not more than half full. Make sure there's enough liquid. If there isn't enough, then you won't get steam and that's what builds up the pressure in the pressure cooker. A recipe should always have at least ½ cup (120 ml) of liquid. If the pressure cooker is having a hard time coming up to full pressure, take it off the heat or turn it off. Carefully release the pressure and add another ¼ cup (60 ml) of liquid and continue. An electronic pot will let you know it's not coming up to full pressure and a stovetop version won't start to whistle. Fried chicken takes a very long time to cook, but resist the urge to deep fry anything under pressure. The oil can melt a gasket and be very dangerous.

Quick pressure release is a cool feature of the new electronic models and allows you to . . . well, release the pressure quickly. This shortens the cooking time, which is important if you are making something that could go mushy in the 10 to 20 minutes or so it would take for the pressure to dissipate naturally—think veggies or pasta. There is a release valve that will allow the steam to quickly dissipate. Make sure you keep your hands and face clear of it. Steam burns can be bad! It's hotter than boiling water.

Natural pressure release happens . . . well, naturally. When the pressure cooker is removed from the heat or the timer goes off, the pressure cooker may turn off or go into a warming function where the pressure is released gradually over the next 10 to 20 minutes. You want to also use this technique if the ingredients are prone to foaming. A full pot of oatmeal or soup can foam up (even if you followed the rule of not filling it more than two-thirds full); if it has bubbled up near the valve when it's released, then bits of it can be forced up through the valve, making a sputtering mess and potentially clogging up the valve. This is also a good technique to use for large cuts of meat. Think of it as a built-in resting period that will give you extra-tender, luscious pieces of meat. The key to comedy and pressure cooking is . . . timing.

Cut your ingredients so that they are sized the same. This will enable them to cook at the same rate. And think about what you're putting in the pot. If it takes you longer to make brown rice on the stovetop, it's going to take longer in the pressure cooker too. Don't be skittish about cutting down cooking times. After a quick release, it's easy to check the status of your food by taking a peek. You can always bring it back up to pressure.

Troubleshooting Pressure Cooking

Having some issues? Make sure your stovetop pressure cooker is being exposed to the highest level of heat from your stovetop until you reach pressure. Don't lower the heat until you hear that whistle and the steam starts to come out—that means you've reached pressure and can lower the heat so that little or no steam is escaping. The pressure cooker won't open until the pressure has gone back down. I can't imagine anyone trying to force a pressure cooker open. That's nuts. It will automatically loosen when it's ready to be opened safely. You can run cool water over the top of a stovetop model or hit a quick release valve to release the steam before opening on an electric model.

If there's loads of steam still escaping, then you probably need to look at your manual and clean the gasket, which may involve taking it apart and then reassembling.

If your food is taking too long to cook, add less liquid next time and make sure you aren't putting anything frozen in there that would slow it down.

Perfect Pork Carnitas

From tacos to grits, this succulent bit of heaven is good on just about everything. We're using a cheap but oh so flavorful cut of meat again, which would normally take a very long time to break down—say 6 to 8 hours—but it will be done in just a little over an hour in our pressure cooker.

SERVES: 8

5-lb (2.25-kg) pork butt roast

1½ tbsp (23 g) salt

1 tbsp (2 g) dried oregano

1 tbsp (7.5 g) ground cumin

1 tsp ground black pepper

½ tsp chili powder

1 onion, quartered

4 cloves garlic, lightly smashed

1 bay leaf

1 cup (235 ml) fresh orange juice

Trim any excess fat from the pork butt, cut into 1-inch (2.5-cm) strips and place in the pressure cooker.

Combine the salt, oregano, cumin, pepper and chili powder together in a bowl. Sprinkle over the pork and stir to evenly coat the meat. Add in the onion, garlic, bay leaf and orange juice.

Lock the lid on the pressure cooker and bring to full pressure over medium heat for 60 minutes. The pork should no longer be pink in the middle and should pull apart easily with forks. Remove the pork from the pressure cooker and continue to shred. Discard the bay leaf.

Bodacious Black Beans

No need to soak dried beans or eat salty, mushed canned beans when you have a pressure cooker. These are by far the best beans!

SERVES: 6–8

7 cups (1.6 L) water

2 tsp (6 g) Better Than Bouillon Roasted Chicken Base

1 lb (454 g) dried black beans

1 small onion, diced

1 bunch cilantro, bound with kitchen string

1 tsp salt

1 bay leaf

1 tbsp (15 ml) extra-virgin olive oil

2 tbsp (30 ml) apple cider vinegar or balsamic vinegar

Place everything except the vinegar in the base of a pressure cooker and stir to combine. Seal the lid and cook at high pressure for 40 minutes.

Release the steam and stir in the vinegar. The beans should be tender and unctuous. Taste to season. Remove the cilantro and bay leaf and serve.

Speedy Spanish Rice

Cooking rice is my Achilles' heel. I don't have the patience for it. I always burn some on the bottom or get nervous there wasn't enough water and end up with total mush. A pressure cooker can make foolproof perfect rice *in half the time!*

SERVES: 6–8

1 tbsp (15 ml) canola oil

1 onion, chopped

2 cups (421 g) medium- or long-grain rice

1 cup (161 g) canned chopped tomatoes

2½ cups (592 ml) water

1 tsp Better Than Bouillon Roasted Chicken Base

2 tsp (10 g) salt

1 tsp dried oregano

Pinch of cayenne pepper

Coat the bottom of the pressure cooker with the oil and add the onion to sauté (if using an Instant Pot, do this in a small sauté pan) until the onions begin to soften and start to get a little color. Add the rice and stir to coat.

In a sauté pan, combine the tomatoes, water, bouillon, salt, oregano and cayenne. Stir to dissolve the bouillon and salt. Pour it all into the pressure cooker, seal and cook for 5 minutes at high pressure. Turn off the heat and allow the pressure cooker to sit for 10 minutes before releasing the pressure. Taste the rice to make sure it's cooked through. Stir with a fork to fluff and serve.

Pressure Cooker
Chicken Stock *(with Beef and Seafood Variations)*

Stocks are the foundation for myriad dishes and are time-consuming to make at home. Unless you have a pressure cooker, that is! Woohoo! Healthy, rich, flavorful stock in a fraction of the time. Collect and freeze bones instead of discarding them and whip up a batch every couple weeks.

MAKES: 8 cups (1.9 L) stock

Chicken carcass left over from a rotisserie or roasted chicken

1 lb (450 g) chicken wings

½ onion, peeled

1 celery rib, roughly chopped

1 large carrot, roughly chopped

1 bay leaf

Fat pinch of salt

BEEF OR SEAFOOD VARIATION
Replace the chicken ingredients above with either:

1 lb (450 g) roasted beef bones or

2 lb (900 g) whole shrimp with shells still on and any fish heads/bones you have saved up

Place everything into the pressure cooker and cover with filtered water to the 10-cup (2,500-ml) line.

Cover and lock. If using a stovetop pressure cooker, heat until the whistle is loud and then reduce the heat to a light hiss and leave for 90 minutes. If using an Instant Pot, pressure cook at high pressure for 90 minutes. In both cases, after 90 minutes, allow the pressure to naturally decrease by either turning the heat off or switching it to the "keep warm" function for half an hour. This also keeps the stock from spurting up through the pressure valve.

Set a strainer atop a large bowl and start by moving the large piece of chicken to the strainer so it doesn't splash out. Next, pour the stock through. Discard or compost the solids. Allow the stock to cool on the counter for half an hour.

With a large spoon, skim the layer of fat from the top and discard. Portion the stock into sturdy zip-top bags, recycled take-out containers or other sealable containers and refrigerate or freeze for up to 4 months.

Mom's Mongolian Beef

My mom has some truly spectacular dishes in her arsenal. This is definitely one of my absolute favorites. It's perfect for chilly nights where you want something deeply satisfying on the table but only have half an hour.

SERVES: 4–6

2 lb (910 g) flank steak, cut into ¼" (6-mm) strips

Salt and pepper

1 tbsp (15 ml) canola or peanut oil

5 cloves garlic, crushed

½ cup (120 ml) low-salt soy sauce

½ cup (120 ml) water

⅔ cup (145 g) brown sugar

1 tsp minced or grated ginger

2 tbsp (19 g) cornstarch mixed with 3 tbsp (44 ml) water, for slurry

3–4 green onions, sliced

Season the sliced beef with salt and pepper. Heat the oil in a sauté pan over medium heat. Add the beef in batches and brown on both sides. Transfer the browned meat to the pressure cooker or Instant Pot bowl.

Add the crushed garlic to the hot pan until fragrant, about 1 minute. Add the soy sauce, water, brown sugar and ginger. Stir to dissolve the sugar and then add the pan's contents to the pressure cooker. Cook at high pressure for 10 minutes. Quick release the pressure and carefully remove the lid.

Whisk the cornstarch and water mixture in a small bowl until lump free.

Select the simmer option on your Instant Pot or return the lidless pressure cooker to the stovetop to simmer. Add in the cornstarch slurry and stir to thicken. Bring the mixture to a boil to fully activate the thickening power of the cornstarch. After 2 minutes and once thick, stir in the green onions and serve with a bowl of rice.

Bacon-Wrapped Meatloaf

Here's a yummy tip: remember that sauce from Better Than Take-Out Teriyaki Chicken (page 72)? Well, if you stir in ketchup you have a pretty amazing barbecue sauce. Thanks to Melissa Smith for figuring this one out when we were running out in our test kitchen one day. The Instant Pot comes with a removable rack that makes lowering things in incredibly easy. The bacon is cooked on the stovetop just to render some of the fat off.

SERVES: 4*

1 lb (450 g) 85%–90% ground beef

¼ cup (60 ml) milk

1 tsp minced garlic

½ tsp garlic powder

½ cup (90 g) grated Parmesan cheese

1 egg

1 tsp salt

¼ tsp ground pepper

¼ cup (30 g) panko bread crumbs

¼ cup (60 ml) barbecue sauce

6 strips bacon, precooked but not crispy

In a large bowl, combine everything but the barbecue sauce and bacon. Mix thoroughly.

Cut a 20-inch (50-cm) square of foil and fold twice to get a long, strong strip. Shape the meat mixture into a football shape in the middle of the foil. Using a pastry brush, coat the top of the meatloaf with the barbecue sauce and then drape the bacon slices over the top, tucking the ends underneath.

Add 2 cups (473 ml) of water to the bottom of the pressure cooker and lower in the meatloaf using the foil saddle. Lock the top and cook at high pressure for 15 minutes. Quick release the pressure and move the meatloaf to a sheet pan. Coat the bacon with another layer of barbecue sauce and broil for 5 minutes or until it starts to caramelize.

* Feel free to double this recipe for a crowd of 6 to 8; just add 10 minutes to the pressure cooking time.

Chapter 10

That's Cold, Baby

Your Refrigerator Is a Tool

For as much work as it does, the refrigerator doesn't get enough love or respect. Until the power goes off, that is. Suddenly it's like the Ark of the Covenant. A magical box full of promise that we have to keep closed or risk unleashing holy hell—or, you know, precious cold air.

The refrigerator has revolutionized the way we eat. Who here preserves their food? I see one, maybe two hands (okay, they're mine, but I sense a few hands going up out there). It used to be back in Grandpappi's day that everyone had to preserve their food. It was a big part of life. We are lucky to live in a time and country not consumed with fear of what we're about to consume. Foodborne illness was widely prevalent. And indoor plumbing was not. Seriously folks, gilded age we're in.

The Best Tools for the Job

All right, so we've established that food can be kept cold to inhibit the growth of bacteria, but how do we do that? And how cold should it be? Ladies and gentlemen, allow me to introduce you to the Danger Zone. This is the window of temperature where bacteria are comfortable and it is from 40°F to 140°F (4 to 60°C). Think hot tub scene on a reality show comfortable. They get gross really fast. We need to keep them cold so they stop procreating. They need to be kept under 40°F (4°C). If it's a hot food, say a slow cooker of chili at your super bowl party, you need to keep that baby at 140°F (60°C) or higher or risk getting everyone sick. My fear of getting people sick has led me to a certification in food safety from the National Restaurant Association.

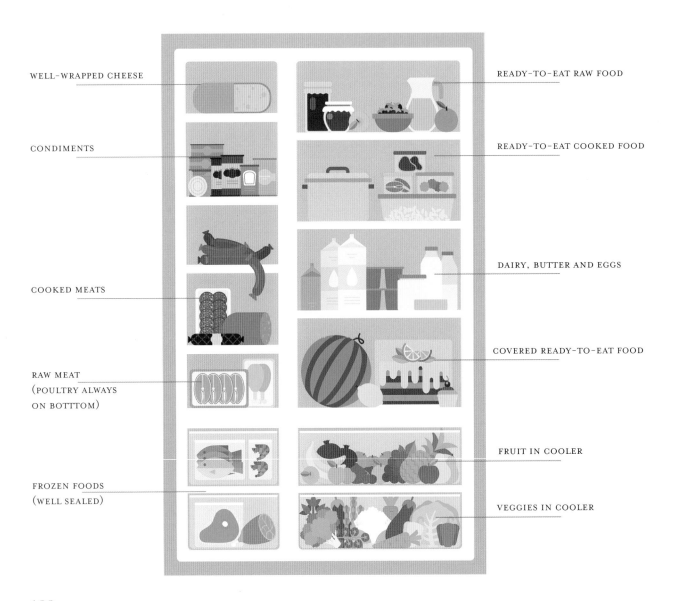

WELL-WRAPPED CHEESE

CONDIMENTS

COOKED MEATS

RAW MEAT
(POULTRY ALWAYS
ON BOTTTOM)

FROZEN FOODS
(WELL SEALED)

READY-TO-EAT RAW FOOD

READY-TO-EAT COOKED FOOD

DAIRY, BUTTER AND EGGS

COVERED READY-TO-EAT FOOD

FRUIT IN COOLER

VEGGIES IN COOLER

How Do Refrigerators Work?

There are five basic factors to run a refrigerator. There's a compressor that constricts the refrigerator's gas; just like in a pressure cooker, this extra atmospheric pressure actually changes the nature of the gas. The gas gets circulated through the coils you can see on the outside of your refrigerator (or behind a panel of your fancy new refrigerator).

When the gas reaches these room-temperature coils, it becomes a liquid—a liquid that is still under a lot of pressure, which causes it to cool down. This cool liquid drips down and flows into the coils that are inside the fridge and freezer. As it reaches an equilibrium with the temperature inside the fridge, it releases cold and absorbs any heat. Any warmth it absorbs in the fridge causes it to revert back to a gas and flow back into the compressor, where it does it all over again. Make sense? No? Okay, it's a magic box. All hail the magic box.

Make the Fridge Work for You!

As a busy lady, I'm super busy. Busy all the time doing busy lady things, so I'm a big fan of passive activity, things that are working when I'm not. Let's put that magic cold box to work!

Other Tools of the Trade

ZEROLL ICE CREAM SCOOP: Paying $20 for an ice cream scoop sent me into some sort of cheapskate shock, but my husband, who researches everything until he's blue in the face, insisted that this was the absolute best ice cream scooper out there, and you know what? It totally is. It looks old-fashioned, but it's filled with this heat-conductive fluid. Your hand heat actually heats up the scooper. I've scooped a lot of ice cream in my time; leaving the box out to temper or nuking it for 10 seconds is no good. Get one of these babies and it will scoop even the hardest ice cream perfectly right out of the freezer. Don't dishwash it, though! I think that screws up whatever is inside.

GLASS BOWLS AND JARS: Glass is a good choice for dishes made with eggs and acidic ingredients. Metal heats up faster and can react with the acid in citrus juices and tomatoes, giving off a weird metallic taste (or in the case of copper and citrus, poison). Glass heats up more slowly, protecting delicate egg dishes, and won't react with any citrus flavors. It's pretty much the only vessel that won't impart anything at all to what it's holding.

CHEESE BAGS/PAPER: Cheese needs to breath, or it will get moldy fast, but not too much breathing or it will dry out. The perfect amount of moisture, you can handle that, right? I can't and I got sick of throwing away expensive cheese, so I took a chance on cheese storage bags. They're a hybrid of polyethylene and wax-coated paper and they work amazingly well. My cheese keeps significantly longer, well making up for the cost of the bags. The Bee's Wrap wax-coated cotton paper is also great for food storage. Keep the plastic wrap and foil for things that need to be kept airtight.

Tips for the Best Ingredients

How you fill your fridge can greatly affect the longevity of your food. It makes sense that the area by the door will generally be the warmest area in your fridge. Every time the door opens, whatever you have in the door can flirt with the danger zone. Keep it cold! Invest in a little fridge thermometer and keep it toward the front to make sure it never goes above 40°F (4°C).

You may have a door shelf built to hold milk but know that the milk will likely spoil sooner if you keep it here. Push it farther into the fridge, closer to the back and toward the bottom where it's cooler.

Do your berries go funky fast in the crisper? That's because the crisper is a moist environment. It's promoting the funk. Keep berries and ready-to-eat foods at the top. This keeps any rogue raw juices from things about to be cooked from dripping down onto them.

Herbs

In an ideal world, we all don our oversized, glamorous, brimmed straw hats, grab a wooden basket and waft into our garden while singing the *Sound of Music* to pick fresh herbs for that evening's dinner. The reality is (for me at least), I'm lucky to have thought ahead to even having fresh herbs in my fridge, so having them last more than a few days is a boon for that week's meals. To keep them from going black, tear off what you need and store the remaining herbs like so: Super woody rosemary can be stood in a small vase with water and covered on top with a plastic bag. More delicate herbs can get a quick rinse in cool water and then be immediately wrapped in a paper towel. The towel will keep them moist but not soggy. Tuck that paper towel in a zip-top bag, seal it up and label it. Leave it on the top shelf where it will keep well and remain top of mind when you're cooking. Basil is best left on the counter in a vase with water, but if you don't have the space, then the rinse-and-wrap method above should keep it for a day or two. It's worth having a basil plant in your window if possible so you can just pluck off what you need.

Eggs

We plow through eggs in my household. The eggs in the United States have gone through a sanitizer bath to reduce the risk of salmonella and other contaminants. Unfortunately, this also removes the cuticle around the egg. This is a natural barrier that comes from the laying chicken to keep the egg safe from bacteria. Removing this exposes the thousands of pores to odors and flavors from whatever else is in the fridge, so keeping them in a sealed carton or a glass-covered dish will keep them tasting better longer.

Butter and Soft Cheeses

These do very well in the door. Condiments that are usually either very acidic or full of preservatives also can last good and long in the door.

If you prefer your butter spreadable, the salted variety is less likely to become contaminated. Keep it covered in a butter dish.

Fruits and Vegetables

Keep your fruits and veggies separate; don't cram them all into the same crisper door. Fruits can release ethelyne, the gas that causes rapid maturation (does not work on children) and speeds up veggie spoilage.

Meat

Raw meat goes at the very bottom. If you aren't lucky enough to have a meat drawer at the very bottom, then store it on a large plate as close to the bottom as possible to collect any errant juices.

Nuts

Nuts have a lot of unsaturated fats that are prone to going rancid. Keep them in an airtight container in the fridge or freezer and they can last for up to a year.

Tomatoes

Tomatoes should stay on the counter. They go mealy in the fridge and are big ethylene producers. Avocados should also hang out on the counter, unless you have a unicorn avocado. That's an avocado that's perfectly ripe; you can pop that in the fridge to keep it from going overripe too quickly. The same goes for perfectly ripe bananas. Their skin will turn brown, but they'll still be great for eating.

Potatoes & Onions

Potatoes also go mealy in the fridge. Keep them in a brown paper bag somewhere cool and dark. Sprouts can be removed, but if they go green, it's time to toss them. Keep your onions in a cool place too, but not the same place as the potatoes. They'll be a bad influence on each other and deteriorate even faster. Chives and green onions should go in the fridge.

Syrup

This should actually be refrigerated. Cold syrup on pancakes bums me out, so feel free to heat up some on pancake day. It's extra yummy that way because it reduces it some, making the maple taste even more intense. Add a few tablespoons of butter for an even more decadent treat.

Honey

Honey stays in the cabinet. It will crystalize in the fridge. Not a deal breaker, just submerge it in a pot of warm water to bring it back.

Tortillas

These are more delicate than bread, so stick them in the fridge and they'll stay perfect until their expiration date.

Dried Meats and Salami

Once these are open, they should go into the fridge, as they are prone to bacteria.

Troubleshooting Your Fridge

Is that thermometer you diligently hung in your fridge reading a bit too hot? Before you call the repairman, there are a few things you can do yourself. Check the back—your fridge needs a few inches of space behind it for the fans to work properly. Sometimes just scooting it out an inch or two is enough to get it back up to speed.

Check those screens! Just like your dryer, lint and dust can severely diminish its efficacy. Grab a screwdriver to take off any panels at the top or bottom and use a dry scrub brush to brush off any accumulated dust. I've had to do this more than once and the difference is amazing.

Lastly, don't stack food directly in front of the fan in the fridge. Allow the air to flow through and it won't have to work so hard to reach all the shelves and your investment will last longer.

Better Morning Night Oats

What I really love about this chapter is that these are all the recipes I whip out when I have company over. I don't want to spend all my time in the kitchen when we have overnight guests, so to have stuff happening in the fridge makes me feel so accomplished. And it's all pretty good, if I do say so myself. Here's a hearty breakfast to have ready when people start popping up in the morning.

SERVES: 2

⅓ cup (80 g) plain Greek yogurt

½ cup (40 g) rolled oats

⅔ cup (160 ml) milk (feel free to swap in a vegan milk)

1 tbsp (7 g) flax meal

½ tsp vanilla or almond extract

Pinch of salt

2 tbsp (30 ml) maple syrup (optional)

Fresh berries, for serving

Mix all the ingredients together in a medium bowl and spoon into a container with a tight-fitting lid. Close well and refrigerate for at least 4 hours or overnight. Serve with berries.

Avocado and Tuna Ceviche

This is the ultimate appetizer. All the "cooking" gets done in the fridge by the acids in the lime juice. It's so silky and decadent. If you have hungry people, they will devour this. Serve with tortilla chips and stand back. If you need to ripen your avocado quickly, place it in a brown paper bag with a tomato. They both release ethylene, which will promote ripening.

SERVES: 4–6

3 tbsp (28 g) diced red onion

1 clove garlic, minced

1 jalapeño, seeded and diced, to taste

Juice of 2 limes (about $\frac{1}{3}$ cup [80 ml])

$\frac{1}{4}$ cup (60 ml) extra-virgin olive oil

1 ripe avocado, peeled, seeded and diced

1 lb (450 g) fresh yellowfin tuna, cut into $\frac{1}{2}$" (13-mm) dice

$\frac{1}{4}$ cup (10 g) chopped cilantro (optional)

Salt and pepper

Tortilla chips, for serving

Add the onion, garlic, jalapeño, lime juice and olive oil to a medium bowl and mix with a fork to combine. Fold in the avocado, tuna and cilantro (if using), then season with salt and pepper.

Cover with plastic wrap and chill for 15 to 30 minutes. Longer than 30 minutes and the tuna will start to turn grayish (still yummy, though). Serve with tortilla chips.

Cappuccino Panna Cotta

Creamy delicious and no right to be as good as it is considering how little you did to make it. Seriously, we're talking 5 minutes. It will take you longer to decide what flavor to make it.

SERVES: 6–8

¼ cup (50 g) coffee beans

4 cups (945 ml) heavy cream

½ cup (96 g) sugar

4 tsp (10 g) unflavored powdered gelatin

6 tbsp (90 ml) cold water

Whipped cream, for serving

Ground coffee, for garnish

Crush the coffee beans lightly between two bowls and add to a saucepan.

Pour over the heavy cream and sugar and heat over medium heat until the sugar is dissolved. For a more intense coffee flavor, let it steep for 5 minutes.

Sprinkle the gelatin over the water to bloom in a large bowl.

Strain the coffee mixture over the gelatin and stir until completely dissolved. Pour into ramekins and chill for at least 2 hours.

If you would like to serve unmolded, run a paring knife around the edge and invert onto a plate. Top with whipped cream and sprinkle with ground coffee to garnish.

Limoncello Granita

No ice cream machine? No problem. You'll get something more akin to a slushy with a granita. It's completely easy and elegant served in a cocktail glass. Squeeze your own lemons! It's so much better and less expensive. If you use the stuff from the plastic lemons, then we need to have a serious talk.

MAKES: About 1 quart (950 ml)

1¼ cups (240 g) sugar

1½ cups (355 ml) warm water

½ cup (120 ml) fresh lemon juice

3 tbsp (44 ml) limoncello liqueur

Pinch of salt

Lemon zest, for garnish

Combine all of the ingredients in a shallow baking dish. Something like an 8 x 8-inch (20 x 20-cm) glass dish would be perfect. Stir with a fork to dissolve the sugar and place uncovered in the freezer.

After 1 hour undisturbed, take a fork to the mixture. There might not be any ice crystals formed yet. Check back every half hour for ice to begin forming and scrape any up with a fork to create a slush.

If you do have an ice cream maker, then spin as usual for a limoncello sorbet. Garnish individual servings with a sprinkle of lemon zest.

Sweet Pickled Jalapeños

The refrigerator is a wonderful place to start your pickling empire! Every time I've made these, someone tells me I need to stop what I'm doing and start selling jars of this stuff. I'd prefer to just make the occasional jar and raid it when I need a quick snack that wakes me up! Or when I need a secret weapon to make a killer grilled cheese.

MAKES: Approximately 3 cups (450 g)

2 cups (473 ml) apple cider vinegar

3 cups (575 g) sugar

I tbsp (11 g) garlic powder

Small pinch of cayenne pepper

I tsp celery seed

3 lb (1.4 kg) jalapeños, sliced ¼" (6 mm) thick, seeds left in*

In a 3-quart (3-L) saucepot, bring everything but the jalapeños to a boil and stir to dissolve all of the sugar.

Reduce the heat and add the jalapeños. Simmer for 3 minutes, and then turn off the heat.

With a slotted spoon, move the jalapeños to jars and stop just shy of the top, then pour in the hot pickling liquid. Allow the contents to cool for an hour and then place a lid on and store in the fridge for 2 to 3 months.

* It's worth investing in a box of disposable gloves for the kitchen, especially for tasks like dredging raw chicken or cutting up pounds of super-hot jalapeños.

Acknowledgments

Thank you, thank you, thank you, Page Street Publishing. To Will Kiester and Sarah Monroe for thinking that I had a book in me. To Karen Levy and Brittany Wason for helping me find it and get it out. To Kylie Alexander for making it look good. And to Alexandra Grablewski for the most beautiful pictures I could ever hope for.

Thank you to my husband, Eric, for being so wonderfully supportive. My mom, dad and brother for not thinking this whole being-a-chef-thing was crazy. And my small, but amazing, group of friends for laughing at my jokes and keeping me sane. And last, but not least, to the sweetest little boy in the world, Xander, who tells everyone that his mom is a chef, uses a chef's knife with ease and eats most of what I put on the table.

Dedicated to you, hungry for knowledge, hungry for food.

About the Author

Michelle Doll grew up along the East Coast and Midwest as an Army brat. This unique upbringing exposed her to foods from all over the world. She got her first restaurant job at 15, working in the kitchen after school and waitressing (horribly, it's a very hard job—tip better) at a Thai restaurant outside the gates of Fort Leonard Wood, Missouri. After she started dating the son of a pizzeria owner, she started working at a pizzeria in Waynesville, Missouri, where it wasn't uncommon to get a single order for hundreds of pizzas for Army recruits in need of a reward. After college and a few years of finding herself/modeling/going to acting school in New York, she began working in corporate identity development and design as a project manager, implementation director and sometimes graphic designer. She got only the Food Network and NY1 channels on her TV at home in her tiny New York apartment and soon became obsessed with cooking. Sara Moulton, Gale Gand, Jacques Torres and Bobby Flay all lit a fire under her to become a chef. She turned in her corporate power suits for chef whites and attended the French Culinary Institute—the first time she ever heard her name and "graduates with honors" in the same breath. She went on to work for Ron Ben-Israel as a cake artist and later became the owner of her own wedding cake and catering company, Michelle Doll Cakes. Food Network came knocking and she found herself on *Throwdown with Bobby Flay* (she won) and countless *Food Network Challenges* (she failed hilariously). She moved on to become the executive chef of Patisserie Colson for a few years before she started to teach, first at the Center for Kosher Culinary Arts and later for Sur La Table and ultimately her alma mater, the French Culinary Institute—now known as the International Culinary Center. She continues to appear on TV frequently and teach, fully believing any information worth knowing is information worth sharing.

Index